REA's Books Are

They have rescued lots of g....... .... more!

(a sample of the <u>hundreds of letters</u> REA receives each year)

(more on next page)

(continued from previous page)

"Your books have saved my GPA, and quite possibly my sanity. My course grade is now an 'A', and I couldn't be happier."

Student, Winchester, IN

"These books are the best review books on the market. They are fantastic!"

Student, New Orleans, LA

"Your book was responsible for my success on the exam. . . I will look for REA the next time I need help."

Student, Chesterfield, MO

"I think it is the greatest study guide I have ever used!"

Student, Anchorage, AK

"I encourage others to buy REA because of their superiority. Please continue to produce the best quality books on the market."

Student, San Jose, CA

"Just a short note to say thanks for the great support your book gave me in helping me pass the test . . . I'm on my way to a B.S. degree because of you!"

Student, Orlando, FL

JAPANESE FOR BEGINNERS

with CD-ROM

by the Staff of
Research & Education Association

Research & Education Association
61 Ethel Road West
Piscataway, New Jersey 08854

SUPER REVIEW®
OF JAPANESE FOR BEGINNERS with CD-ROM

Year 2005 Printing

Printed in the United States of America

Library of Congress Control Number 2002105282

International Standard Book Number 0-87891-414-5

WHAT THIS Super Review
WILL DO FOR YOU

This Super Review provides all that you need to know to do your homework effectively and succeed on exams and quizzes.

The book focuses on the core aspects of the subject, and helps you to grasp the important elements quickly and easily.

Outstanding Super Review features:

- Lessons are covered in logical sequence

- Lessons are reviewed in a concise and comprehensive manner

- The material is presented in student-friendly form that makes it easy to follow and understand

- For the second part of the book (Lessons 18-36), answers have been provided for the learning exercises

- Provides excellent preparation for midterms, finals and in-between quizzes

- Written by professionals and experts who function as your very own tutors

Larry B. Kling
Super Review Program Director

CONTENTS

Mt. Fuji

101 USEFUL EXPRESSIONS

1. Good morning .... *Ohayo gōzaimas´.*

2. Good day (afternoon) .... *Konnichi-wa.*

3. Good evening .... *Komban-wa.*

4. Good night .... *Oyas´mi-nasai.*

5. Good-bye .... *Sayonara.*

6. How are you? .... *Ikaga des´ ka?*

7. I am well .... *Genki des´.*

8. And you? .... *Anata-wa?*

9. Thank you .... *Arigatō gozaimas´.*

10. Don't mention it .... *Dō itashimash´ te.*

11. It is fine weather, isn't it? .... *Yoi otenki des´, ne.*

12. It is bad weather, isn't it? .... *Warui otenki des´, ne.*

13. Do you speak English? .... *Anata-wa Eigo-ga hanasemas´ ka?*

14. Yes, I speak a little .... *Hai, s´koshi hanasemas´.*

15. No, I do not speak English .... *Iie, Eigo-wa hanasemasen.*

16. Did you understand? .... *Wakarimash´ta ka.*

17. Yes, I understood .... *Hai, wakarimash´ta.*

18. No, I did not understand .... *Iie, wakarimasen desh´ta.*

19. Please say it again .... *Mō ichido itte kudasai.*

20. Please speak slowly .... *Yukkuri hanash´ te kudasai.*

21. I've made a mistake .... *Machigaemash´ta.*

22. Please ....*Dōzo.*

23. Excuse me .... *Gomennasai.*

24. I'm sorry .... *Dōmo sumimasen.*

25. It doesn't matter .... *Kamaimasen.*

26. Hey! (Familiar way of calling attention of someone) .... *Anone.*

27. Excuse me (but may I ask you a question?) .... *Sh´tsurei des´ ga.*

28. Come here, please .... *Koko-e irash´tte kudasai.*

29. Please wait a moment .... *Chotto matte kudasai.*

30. What is your name? .... *Anata-no onamae-wa?*

31. How old are you? .... *Oikuts´ des´ ka?*

32. What shall we do? .... *Dō shimasho ka?*

33. What time is it? .... *Nanji des´ ka?*

34. Is it near? .... *Chikai des´ ka?*

35. Is it far? ....*Tōi des´ ka?*

36. Let's hurry .... *Isogimashō.*

37. What is the matter? .... *Dōshimash´ta ka?*

38. I'm hungry .... *Onaka-ga s´kimash´ta.*

39. I'm thirsty .... *Nodo-ga kawakimash´ta.*

40. I'm tired .... *Ts´karemash´ta.*

41. I'm sleepy .... *Nemui des´.*

42. I'm sick .... *Byōki des´.*

43. Do you like it? .... *S´ki des´ ka?*

44. Yes, I like it .... *Hai, s´ki des´.*

45. No, I don't like it .... *Iie, s´ki dewa arimasen.*

46. It's splendid .... *S´teki des´.*

47. I dislike it .... *Kirai des´.*

48. It's no good .... *Dame des´.*

49. It is very interesting .... *Taihen omoshiroi des´.*

50. It is strange .... *Hen des´.*

51. It is funny (laughable) .... *Okashii des´.*

52. Do you want it? .... *Hoshii des´ ka?*

53. Yes, I want it .... *Hai, hoshii des´.*

54. No, I don't want it .... *Iie, hoshiku arimasen.*

55. What is this? .... *Kore-wa nan des´ ka?*

56. Who is that? .... *Ano hito-wa dare des´ ka?*

57. What is this building? .... *Kono tatemono-wa nan des´ ka?*

58. Please show me .... *Misete kudasai.*

59. Please write it .... *Kaite kudasai.*

60. Please ask .... *Kiite kudasai.*

61. Is that so? .... *Sō des´ ka?*

62. Yes, that is right ....*Hai, sō des´.*

63. No, that is not right .... *Iie, sō dewa arimasen.*

64. That is true .... *Hontō des´.*

65. That is a lie .... *Uso des´.*

66. Oh, I see .... *Aa, sō des´ ka.*

67. Maybe ....*Tabun.*

68. Of course ....*Mochiron.*

69. It is all right... *Daijōbu des´.*

70. Do you know? .... *Sh´tte imas´ ka?*

71. Yes, I know.....................................*Hai, sh´tte imas´.*

72. No, I don't know .... *Iie, shirimasen.*

73. I think so ....*Sō omoimas´.*

74. I don't think so .... *Sō omoimasen.*

75. I've forgotten ....*Wasuremash´ta.*

76. Can you do it? .... *Dekimas´ ka?*

77. Yes, I can do it....................................... *Hai, dekimas´.*

78. No, I can't do it .... *Iie, dekimasen.*

79. Why? .... *Naze des´ ka?*

80. When? ....*Itsu des´ ka?*

81. Where is it? .... *Doko des´ ka?*

82. How much ? .... *Ikura des´ ka?*

83. At what time? .... *Nanji ni des´ ka?*

84. You are wrong .... *Chigaimas´.*

85. This is plenty .... *Mō tak´san des´.*

86. A little more .... *Mō s´koshi.*

87. Quick! .... *Hayaku!*

88. Look out! .... *Abunai!*

89. It's nothing .... *Nan demo nai.*

90. At once .... *Sugu ni.*

91. Never... *Kessh´te.*

92. Sometimes .... *Tokidoki.*

93. Often .... *Tabitabi.*

94. Go straight ahead .... *Massugu oide nasai.*

95. Turn to the right .... *Migi-e omagari nasai.*

96. Go to the left .... *Hidari-e oide nasai.*

97. Congratulations .... *Omedetō gozaimas´.*

98. Let's go.. *Ikimashō.*

99. Hand me that .... *Are o totte kudasai.*

100. Give me this .... *Kore o kudasai.*

101. I must go (take leave)....................... *Wata´shi-wa mo kaerimasu.*

Important Signs in Japanese

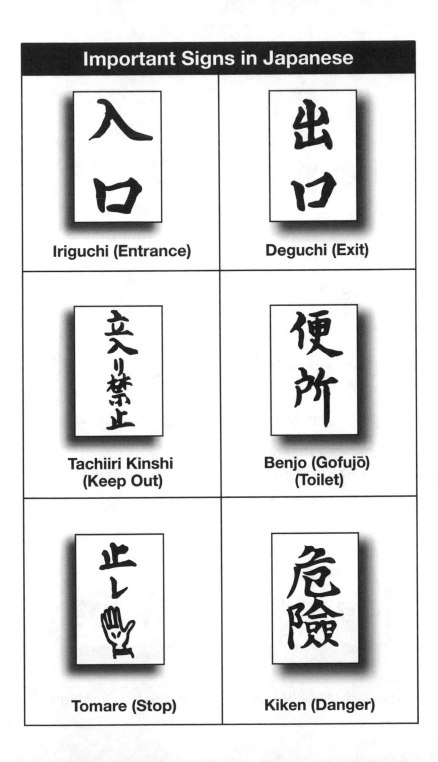

入口
Iriguchi (Entrance)

出口
Deguchi (Exit)

立入り禁止
**Tachiiri Kinshi
(Keep Out)**

便所
**Benjo (Gofujō)
(Toilet)**

止レ
Tomare (Stop)

危険
Kiken (Danger)

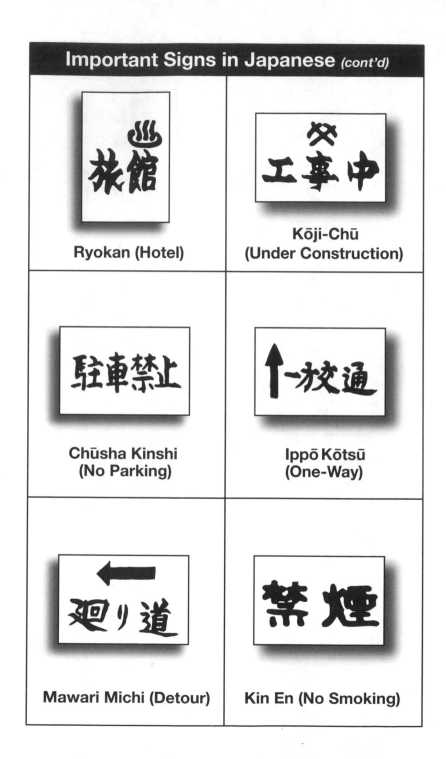

Ryokan (Hotel)

**Kōji-Chū
(Under Construction)**

**Chūsha Kinshi
(No Parking)**

**Ippō Kōtsū
(One-Way)**

Mawari Michi (Detour)

Kin En (No Smoking)

LESSON 1

Kore-wa hon des´.
This is a book.

EXAMPLES

1. **Kore-wa empits´ des´.**
   This is a pencil.

2. **Kore-wa kami des´.**
   This is paper.

3. **Kore-wa ts´kue des´.**
   This is a desk.

4. **Kore-wa isu des´.**
   This is a chair.

5. **Kore-wa kaban des´.**
   This is a briefcase.

6. **Kore-wa bōshi des´.**
   This is a hat.

NOTES

Wa is used to single out a word about which a statement is made. It usually follows the subject of the sentence. It may be best translated "as for" (Speech Pattern 1).

VOCABULARY

bōshi .... *hat; cap*	*kore* .... *this*
kaban .... *briefcase; a satchel; suitcase; traveling-bag*	*empits´ (empitsu)* .. *pencil*
	ts'kue (tsukue) .... *desk*
chōmen .... *notebook*	*hako* .... *box*
kami .... *paper*	*wa* .... *a particle which usually follows the subject of a sentence*
des´ (desu) ..... *am; is; are*	
isu .... *chair*	

LESSON 2

Kore-wa hon des´ ka?
Is this a book?

Kore-wa hon dewa arimasen.
This is not a book.

EXAMPLES

1. **Kore-wa isu des´ ka?**
    Is this a chair?

2. **Iie, sore-wa isu dewa arimasen.**
    No, that is not a chair.

3. **Kore-wa kaban des´ ka?**
    Is this a briefcase?

4. **Iie, sore-wa kaban dewa arimasen.**
    No, that is not a briefcase.

5. **Are-wa bōshi des´ ka?**
    Is that (over there) a hat?

6. Iie, are-wa bōshi dewa arimasen.
No, that (over there) is not a hat.

NOTES

1. *Ka* denotes a question. Any statement can be turned into a question by adding *ka* at the end, without any other change (Speech Pattern 2).

2. *Dewa arimasen* is the negative of *des´*. In rapid, familiar speech *dewa* usually becomes *ja* (Speech Pattern 3).

3. In English a person or thing is referred to by using the words "this" and "that." Japanese has a three-step system in words of this kind. *Kore* refers to what is close to the speaker; *sore* refers to what is a little removed, or what is close to the person spoken to; *are* refers to what is distant.

VOCABULARY

are .... *that (over there)*

dewa arimasen ..... *am not; is not; are not.*

iie .... *no*

inu .... *dog*

ka .... *a particle which denotes a question*

k´tsu (kutsu) .... *shoes*

mannenhitsu .... *fountain pen*

megane .... *spectacles*

neko .... *cat*

saifu .... *purse; pocketbook; wallet*

sore .... *that*

tēburu .... *table*

EXERCISES

1. Make questions and answers in as many combinations as possible using all the words you have learned.

2. Ask your friend to identify what you have, he has, or someone else has, using as many words as you know.

3. Ask your friend questions in affirmative sentences in such a way that he must answer in the negative.

Kore-wa hon des´.

Kore-wa empits´ des´.°

Kore-wa kami des´.

Kore-wa ts´kue des´.

Kore-wa isu des´.

Kore-wa hako des´.

Kore-wa kaban des´.

Kore-wa bōshi des´.

Geisha

Confucian temple

SPEECH PATTERN 4:

Kore-wa sh´roi hon des´.
This is a white book.

SPEECH PATTERN 5:

Kore-wa sh´roi des´.
This is white.

EXAMPLES

1. **Kore-wa ōkii sakana des´.**
    This is a big fish.

2. **Sore-wa chiisai ie des´.**
    That is a small house.

3. **Are-wa atarashii des´.**
    That (over there) is new.

4. **Sore-wa uts´kushii hana des´.**
    Those are beautiful flowers.

5. **Kore-wa ōkii heya des´.**
    This is a large room.

6. **Sore-wa omoi des´.**
   That is heavy.

NOTES

1. All words ending in *i* (with the exception of *ei*) which describe or modify another word (true adjectives) are placed before the words they describe or modify (Speech Pattern 4).

2. True adjectives may also be used alone, that is, without the name of something (noun) following them (Speech Pattern 5).

VOCABULARY

atarashii .... *new, fresh*	*kuroi* .... *black*
chiisai .... *small; little (not big)*	*mijikai* .... *short*
	nagai .... *long*
donna .... *what kind of?*	*ōkii* .... *large, big*
hai .... *yes*	
	omoi .... *heavy*
hana .... *flower*	
	sakana .... *fish*
heya .... *room*	
	semai .... *narrow; small in area*
hiroi .... *broad; wide; large in area*	
	shiroi .... *white*
ie .... *house*	
	uts´kushii
karui .... *light (in weight)*	*(utsukushii)* .... *beautiful*

EXERCISES

1. Make ten questions and answers in Japanese, five to be answered affirmatively and five negatively, for example:

Q: Sore-wa atarashii kaban des´ ka?
Is that a new briefcase?

A: Hai, kore-wa atarashii kaban des´.
Yes, this is a new briefcase.

Q: Kore-wa omoi hako des´ ka?
Is this a heavy box?

A: Iie, sore-wa omoi hako dewa arimasen.
No, that is not a heavy box.

2. Make ten answers in Japanese to the question **Kore-wa donna _____ des´ ka?** (*"What kind of _____ is this?"*), filling in the blank with the nouns you know, for example:

Q: Kore-wa donn hako des´ ka?
What kind of box is this?

A. Sore-wa ōkii hako des´.
That is a big box.

Kore wa isu des´ ka?	Kore wa kaban des´ ka?
Iie, sore-wa isu dewa arimasen. Sore-wa tēburu des´.	Iie, sore-wa kaban dewa arimasen. Sore-wa hako des´.

Kore wa bōshi des´ ka?	Kore wa hon des´ ka?
Hai, sore-wa bōshi des´.	Hai, sore-wa hon des´.

Kore wa hon des´ ka?	Kore wa hon des´ ka?
Sore-wa k´tsu des´.	Sore-wa megane des´.

Kore wa hon des´ ka?	Kore wa hon des´ ka?
Sore-wa inu des´.	Sore-wa neko des´.

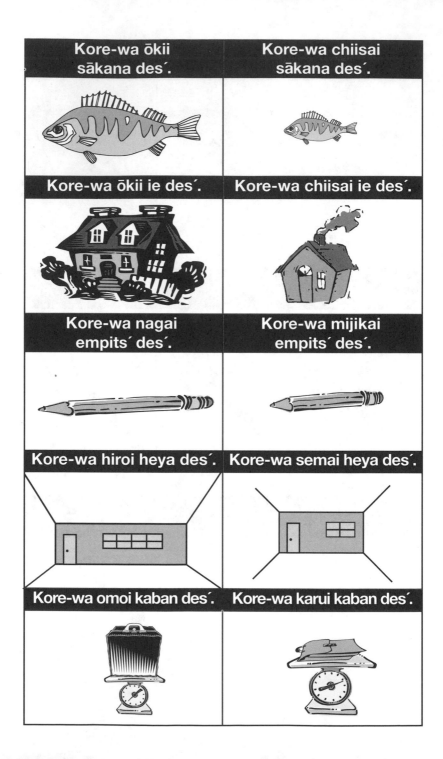

SPEECH PATTERN 6:

Kono hon-wa sh´roi des´.
This book is white.

EXAMPLES

1. **Sono k´tsu-wa atarashii des´.**
   Those shoes are new.

2. **Ano michi-wa ii des´ ka?**
   Is that road (over there) good?

3. **Ano hito-wa sensei dewa arimasen.**
   That person (over there) is not a teacher.

4. **Kono empitsu´-wa mijikai des´.**
   This pencil is short.

5. **Sono hito-wa heitai des´.**
   That person is a soldier.

6. **Ano hito-wa Tanaka-san des´ ka?**
   Is that person (over there) Mr. Tanaka?

NOTES

1. *Kono, sono,* and *ano* correspond to *kore, sore,* and *are.* When they are used to mean "this" or "that," they never stand alone. They always stand immediately before a noun (Speech Pattern 6).

2. The words "he" and "she" are not usually expressed in the Japanese sentence; but when it is necessary, for contrast or clearness, to mention some third party, the most common expressions are *ano hito* and *sono hito* ("that person"). *Ano hito* is used when the person is first referred to, but *sono hito* is used thereafter. *Kata* is the polite way of referring to a person spoken about. It is used for a person to whom respect is to be paid.

3. *Wata´shi* ("I") and *anata* ("you") are used only when they are really necessary to make the sentence clear.

4. *San* is used after a person's name. It often, but not always, corresponds to the English "Mr.," "Mrs.," or "Miss." It should never be used after one's own name, since it is a mark of respect.

5. *Otoko* and *onna* mean respectively "male" and "female." They are commonly used with the particle *no* and a noun; for example: *Otoko no hito* means "man" (male person). They may also be used by themselves to mean respectively "a male," "a man" and "a female," "a woman."

VOCABULARY

akai .... red	*michi* .... road, street
akambo .... baby	*midori* .... green
anata .... you	*no* .... particle used with a noun which modifies another noun (Lesson 6)
ano .... that (over there)	
aoi .... blue	*onna* .... female; a woman
Amerika .... America	*otoko* .... male; a man
furui .... old (of things)	*san* .... a particle usually meaning Mr., Mrs., Miss
hata .... flag	*shashinki* .... camera
hito (kata) .... person	*sono* .... that
hitobito .... people	*takai* .... expensive; high
ii (yoi) .... good	*warui* .... bad
kiiroi .... yellow	*wata'shi (watakushi)* I
kodomo .... child	*yasui* ... inexpensive; cheap
kono .... this	*yoi (ii)* .... good

EXERCISES

1. Express in Japanese as many sentences as possible using the following tables:

a.

	is	
This	red	hat
That	white	book
That (over there)	blue	pencil

b.

		is
This	camera	good
That	house	cheap
That (over there)	fountain pen	expensive

2. Substitute other words you know in the tables and make as many sentences as possible.

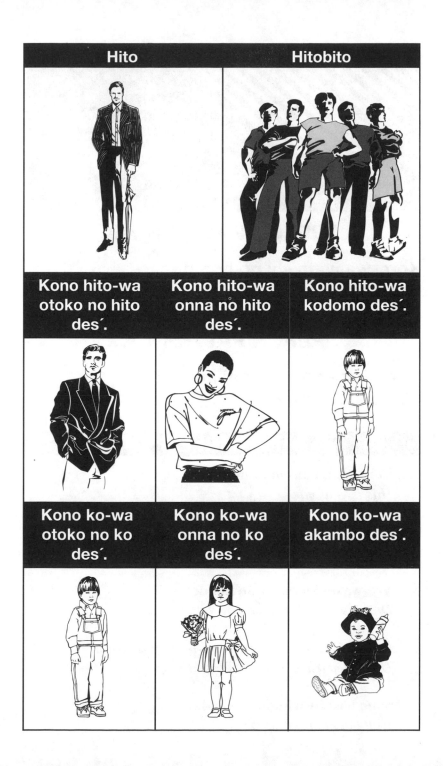

Hito	Hitobito

Kono hito-wa otoko no hito des´.

Kono hito-wa onna no hito des´.

Kono hito-wa kodomo des´.

Kono ko-wa otoko no ko des´.

Kono ko-wa onna no ko des´.

Kono ko-wa akambo des´.

SPEECH PATTERN 7A:

Kore-wa wata´shi no hon des´.
This is my book.

SPEECH PATTERN 7B:

Kono hon-wa wata´shi no des´.
This book is mine.

EXAMPLES

1. **Kore-wa anata-no jidōsha des´.**
   This is your car.

2. **Kore wa ano hito no jiten sha des´.**
   This is his (her) bicycle.

3. **Are-wa otoko no ko-no inu des´.**
   That (over there) is the boy's dog.

4. **Kono kaban-wa Tanaka-san-no dewa arimasen.**
   This briefcase is not Mr. Tanaka's.

5. **Sono bōshi-wa kodomo-no des´.**
   That hat is the child's.

6. Are-wa dare-no ie des´ ka?

Whose house is that (over there)?

NOTES

Possession in Japanese is indicated by the addition of the particle *no* to the word denoting the possessor (Speech Pattern 7 A&B). This *no* has the function similar to the English "'s. "

VOCABULARY

dare (donata) .... *who*	*namae* .... *name*
jidōsha ..... *automobile; car*	*no* .... *particle indicating possession*
jitensha .... *bicycle*	

EXERCISES

1. Make as many sentences as possible in Japanese, using the following tables:

a.

		is (are)
This (these)	my	pocketbook(s)
That (those)	your	spectacles
That (those) (over there)	his (her)	desk(s)

b.

		is not
This	car	mine
That	bicycle	yours
That (over there)	table	his (hers)

2. Make ten questions and answers in Japanese, using *dare-no* ("whose"); for example:

Q: Kore-wa dare-no empits´ des´ ka?
Whose pencil is this?

A: Sono empits´-wa wata´shi-no des´.
That pencil is mine.

SPEECH PATTERN 8:

A. Kore-wa ki-no hako des´.
This is a wooden box.

B. Kore-wa jōbu-na hako des´.
This is a strong box.

EXAMPLES

1. **Kore-wa kami-no hako des´.**
   This is a paper box.

2. **Sore-wa Nihon-no hon des´.**
   That is a Japanese book.

3. **Kono machi-no eki-wa ōkii des´.**
   This town's station is big. (The station in this town is big.)

4. **Ano ko-wa rikō-na seito des´.**
   That boy (over there) is a clever pupil.

5. **Sore-wa kirei-na hana des´.**
   Those are pretty flowers.

6. Kesa-no shimbun-wa omoshiroi des´.
This morning's newspaper is interesting.

NOTES

1. Often there is no meaning of possession involved with the use of *no*. The words which precede the *no* in this case are usually names of countries, materials, time, and place. They are used to identify or describe other nouns (Speech Pattern 8A).

2. If the modifying word is abstract (a quality), *na* is used instead of *no* (Speech Pattern 8B). When these words do not precede the word they modify, the *na* is dropped; for example, *Sono hana-wa kirei des´,* ("Those flowers are pretty"). Example 5 shows the same word (*kirei*) used with *na*.

3. The name of any language is made by adding go to the name of the country; for example, *Chūgokugo* means "Chinese language," (*Chūgoku,* "China" plus *go*, language).

4. The name of the people of a country is made by adding *jin* to the name of the country; for example, *Roshiyajin* means "Russian," (*Roshiya,* "Russia" plus *jin*, "Native").

VOCABULARY

Amerikajin .... *American*	*eki* .... *railroad station*
Eigo .... *English (language)*	*go* .... *suffix meaning "language"*
Igirisu .... *England*	
	jin .... *suffix meaning "native person"*
Igirisujin .... *Englishman*	

VOCABULARY *(cont'd)*

jōbu .... strong; healthy; sturdy

jōzu .... skillful; good at

kesa .... this morning

ki .... tree

ki-no .... wooden

kirei ..... pretty; fine looking

kisha .... steam-train

machi .... town

Nihon (Nippon) .... Japan

Nihongo (Nippongo) .... Japanese *(language)*

Nihonjin (Nipponjin) .... Japanese *(native)*

omoshiroi .... interesting, entertaining

rikō .... clever; wise

Roshiya .... Russia

Roshiyago .... Russian *(language)*

Roshiyajin .... Russian *(native)*

seito .... pupil

shimbun .... newspaper

Chūgoku .... China

Chūgokugo .... Chinese *(language)*

Chūgokujin .... Chinese *(native)*

yowai ...... weak; unhealthy

zasshi .... magazine

EXERCISES

1. Write in Japanese (Romaji):

a. **This is a wooden chair.**

b. **That is this morning's newspaper.**

c. **That is a pretty baby.**

d. **That box (over there) is strong.**

e. **That woman is a Russian.**

f. **The Japanese language is interesting.**

2. Fill in the blanks in the following sentence with *no* or *na:*

a. Kore-wa Chūgoku _____ shimbun des´.

b. Otoko _____ ko _____ bōshi-wa takai des´.

c. Sore-wa kirei _____ akambō des´.

d. Are-wa jobu _____ otoko _____ ko des´.

Kono hito-wa jōbu-na hito des´.

Kono hito-wa yowai hito des´.

Kore-wa Amerika no kisha des´.

Kore-wa Nihon-no kisha des´.

Kore-wa ki-no hako des´.

Kore-wa kami-no hako des´.

SPEECH PATTERN 9:

Kore-wa sh´roku arimasen.
This is not white.

EXAMPLES

1. **Kore-wa yas´ku arimasen.**
   This is not cheap.

2. **Sono ie-wa ōkiku arimasen.**
   That house is not big.

3. **Kono jidōsha-wa takaku arimasen.**
   This car is not expensive.

4. **Kono kodomo-wa chiisaku arimasen.**
   This child is not small.

5. **Ano ts´kue-wa yoku arimasen.**
   That desk (over there) is not good.

6. **Kore-wa muzukash´ku arimasen.**
   This is not difficult.

NOTES

When adjectives are used in negative sentences such as Speech Pattern 9, the final *i* of the modifying word must be changed to *ku* and *arimasen* added. It is optional to use *wa* before *arimasen* (Speech Pattern 9). Adjectives used with *na* do not change for the negative.

VOCABULARY

atatakai .... *warm*	*samai* .... *cold (weather)*
atsui .... *hot (weather)*	*suzushii* ...... *cool (weather)*
muzukashii .... *difficult*	*yasashii* .... *easy*

EXERCISES

1. Review all the modifying words you have had and change them into their negative forms.

2. Change sentences made in exercises in Lesson 6 to negative.

Hokkaido

Shinto Shrine

SPEECH PATTERN 10:

Kore-wa atarashii des´ ka, furui des´ ka?
Is this new or old?

EXAMPLES

1. **Haru-wa atatakai des´ ka, suzushii des´ ka?**
   Is spring warm or cool?

2. **Natsu-wa atsui des´ ka, samui des´ ka?**
   Is summer hot or cold?

3. **Ima-wa aki des´ ka, fuyu des´ ka?**
   Is it autumn or winter now?

4. **Anata-wa sensei des´ ka, seito des´ ka?**
   Are you a teacher or a student?

5. **Kore-wa kabe des´ ka, tenjō des´ ka?**
   Is this a wall or a ceiling?

6. **Sono junsa-no jidōsha-wa akai des´ ka, kuroi des´ ka?**
   Is that policeman's car red or black?

NOTES

When a question is asked about the state or identity of something and alternatives are given for the possible answer, *ka* is used after each choice (Speech Pattern 10).

VOCABULARY

aki .... *autumn*	*kabe* .... *wall*
asa .... *morning*	*mado* .... *window*
ban .... *evening*	*natsu* .... *summer*
dentō .... *electric light*	*sensei* .... *teacher*
e .... *painting; drawing; picture*	*tenjo* .... *ceiling*
fuyu .... *winter*	*to* .... *door*
haru .... *spring (season)*	*yoru* .... *night*
hiru .... *noon*	*yūgata* .... *early evening*
ima .... *now*	*yuka* .... *floor*

EXERCISES

1. Using Speech Pattern 10, make questions concerning the identity of items in the drawing of a room (Example 5).

2. Using Speech Pattern 10, make questions in Japanese concerning the state of as many things as you know (Example 6).

LESSON 9

REVIEW LESSON

A. Review the ten speech patterns. Say them from memory. Make two sentences of each pattern substituting words in the different sentence elements.

B. Review the five particles. Make two sentences illustrating the use of each particle.

C. Review the three-step system of words which point out persons and things. Make two sentences using each one with *wa* and two sentences using each with a noun.

D. Review all the modifying words (adjectives) you have had and give the positive and negative form of each.

VOCABULARY

chawan .... *cup*

chōchin .... *Japanese paper lantern*

dobin .... *tea kettle*

Fujisan .... *Mt. Fuji*

gojūnōto .... *five-story pagoda*

hashi .... *chopsticks*

VOCABULARY *(cont'd)*

heitai .... *soldier*	**kushi** .... *comb*
hōki .... *broom*	**omiya** .... *shrine*
isha .... *medical doctor*	**sakura** .... *cherry-blossom*
jochū .... *housemaid*	**suihei** .... *sailor*
junsa .... *policeman*	**torii** .... *gateway identifying the approach to a Shinto Shrine*
kama .... *rice boiler*	
kasa .... *umbrella*	**tōrō** .... *stone or metal lantern*

EXERCISES

1. Make five questions requiring affirmative answers in Japanese identifying the objects on page 49, and five requiring negative answers; for example:

Q: Kore-wa hōki des´ ka?
Is this a broom?

A: Hai, sore-wa hōki des´.
Yes, that is a broom.

Q: Kore-wa torii des´ ka?
Is this a torii?

A: Iie, sore-wa torii dewa arimasen.
No, that is not a torii.

2. Make five questions and answers identifying people, for example:

Q: Ano hito-wa dare des´ ka?
Who is that person (over there)?

A: Ano hito-wa junsa des´
That person (over there) is a policeman.

3. Express in Japanese:

a. This is a small (in area) room.

b. This is a pretty picture (painting).

c. That man is skillful.

d. That car (over there) is not expensive.

e. This is Mr. Kimura's hat.

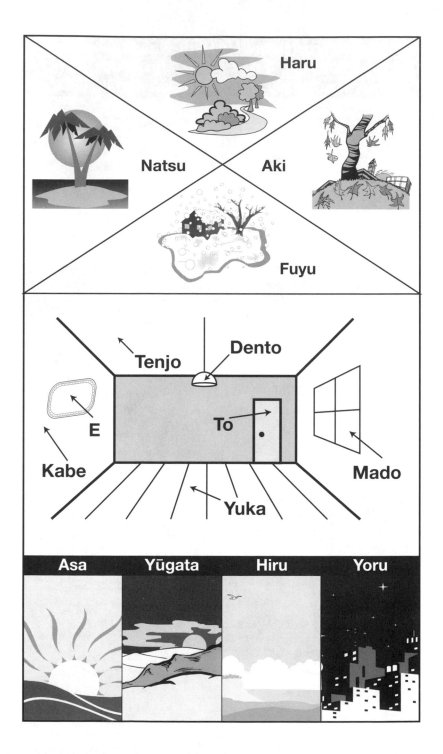

Fujisan

Sakura

Torii

Gojūnotō

Omiya

Tōrō

Kasa

Hōki

Dobin

Kama

Chawan

Chōchin

Hashi

Kushi

Kono hito-wa sensei des´. Kono hito-wa isha des´.

Kono hito-wa seito des´.

Kono hito-wa jochū des´. Kono hito-wa junsa des´.

Kono hito-wa heitai des´. Kono hito-wa suihei des´.

SPEECH PATTERN 11:

Hon-wa ts'kue no ue ni arimas´.
The book is on the desk.

EXAMPLES

1. **Megane-wa tēburu no ue ni arimas´.**
   The spectacles are on the table.

2. **Hako-wa tēburu no sh´ta ni arimas´.**
   The box is under the table.

3. **Mado-wa ts´kue no ushiro ni arimas´.**
   The window is behind the desk.

4. **Isu-wa ts´kue no mae ni arimas´.**
   The chair is in front of the desk.

5. **Kaban-wa ie no naka ni arimas´.**
   The briefcase is in the house.

6. **Ki-wa ie no soba ni arimas´.**
   The tree is near the house.

NOTES

1. *Ni* denotes the place where a thing is to be found or exists. It often follows a specific place word. To say "on the desk" one must think of it as "on the desk's top" or *ts´kue no ue ni* (Speech Pattern 11).

2. The Japanese language makes a distinction between living things and lifeless things. For people, animals, insects, etc., *imas´* is used to mean "to be," "to exist," "to lie," "there is (are)," etc., while for buildings, furniture, utensils, trees, plants, etc. — things which cannot change their position by their own strength — *arimas´* is used.

VOCABULARY

aida (ni) .... *between*	*shindai* .... *bed*
dai .... *stand, as meaning "piece of furniture"*	*sh'ta (shita) (ni)* ...... *under*
mae .... *front*	*soba (ni)* .... *near*
naka .... *inside*	*ue (ni)* .... *on; above*
ni .... *to; in; on; at*	*ushiro (ni)* .... *rear; behind*

EXERCISES

1. Express in Japanese as many sentences as possible from the following table:

	is	
book	on	table
box	under	chair
briefcase	in front of	desk
cap	by	stand
wallet	behind	bed

2. Write the following sentences in Japanese:

a. **The bed is between the window and the stand.**

b. **The bicycle is between the tree and the house.**

c. **The pencil is between the magazine and the newspaper.**

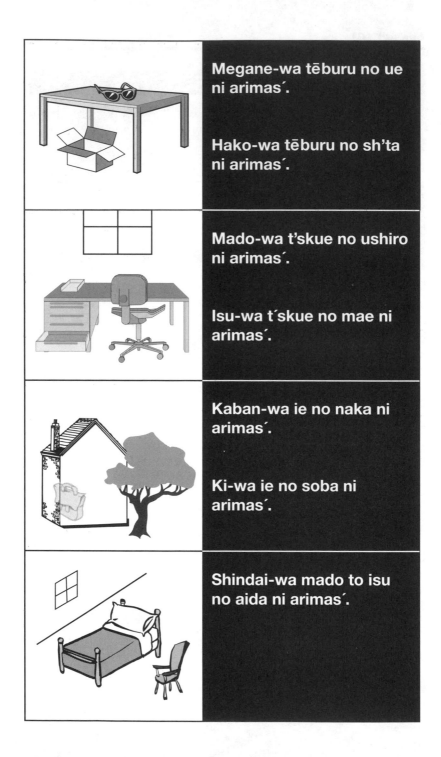

Megane-wa tēburu no ue ni arimas´.

Hako-wa tēburu no sh'ta ni arimas´.

Mado-wa t'skue no ushiro ni arimas´.

Isu-wa t´skue no mae ni arimas´.

Kaban-wa ie no naka ni arimas´.

Ki-wa ie no soba ni arimas´.

Shindai-wa mado to isu no aida ni arimas´.

"Narumi," Ando Hiroshige

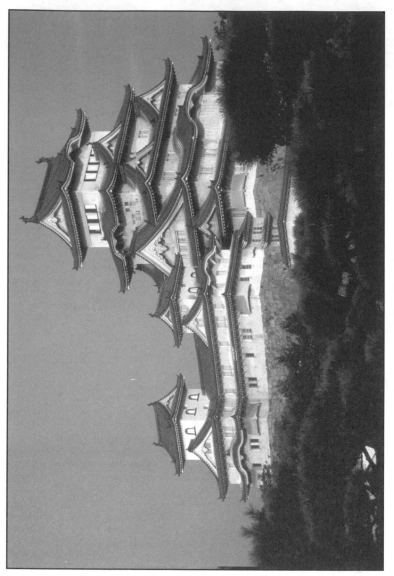

Himeji castle

LESSON 11

SPEECH PATTERN 12:

Ie no naka ni inu-ga imas´.
There is a dog in the house.

EXAMPLES

1. **Hako no naka ni nani-ga imas´ ka?**
   What (living) is in the box?

2. **Hako no naka ni tori-ga imas´.**
   There is a bird in the box.

3. **Kodomo-wa doko ni imas´ ka?**
   Where are the children?

4. **Kodomo-wa gakkō ni imas´.**
   The children are in school.

5. **Kisha no naka ni inu-ga imas´.**
   There is a dog in the train.

6. **Kono machi ni wa Amerika no heitai-ga imas´.**
   There are American soldiers in this town.

NOTES

1. A more polite word to use in place of *imas'* to indicate the position or existence of living things is *orimas'*. Both words can be used interchangeably.

2. Since *wa* and *ga* are used after the subject of a sentence, the difference between the two is one of the puzzling problems in learning Japanese. The fundamental difference between the two lies in the emphasis placed on the words which precede them. *Wa* is ordinarily used with the subject; however, *ga* has a stronger tone, giving particular emphasis to the subject, or pointing out a particular one out of many.

3. *Wa* is used after words denoting location or time where that particular location or time is singled out from among other possible locations or times (See Example 6).

VOCABULARY

asoko .... *that place (over there)*

doko ..... *what place; where*

ga .... *particle which emphasizes the subject*

gakkō .... *school*

hidari .... *left*

koko .... *this place; here*

massugu .... *straight*

migi .... *right (direction)*

ryōriya .... *restaurant (large Japanese)*

soko .... *that place; there*

tansu .... *chest of drawers*

te .... *hand*

tori .... *bird*

yoko .... *side*

EXERCISES

1. Referring to the first sketch on page 61, express each of the following questions in Japanese and give the proper answers:

a. **What is under the tree?**

b. **What is at the right of the tree?**

c. **What is at the left of the tree?**

d. **What is behind the tree?**

2. Referring to the second sketch on page 61, express each of the following questions in Japanese and give the proper answers:

a. What is in front of the station?

b. What is behind the station?

c. What is above the restaurant?

d. What is in front of the restaurant?

Ts´kue-no ue ni nani-ga arimas´ ka? Ts´kue-no ue ni hon-ga arimas´.	Hako-no naka ni nani-ga imas´ ka? Hako-no naka ni tori-ga imas´.

Hon-wa doko ni arimas´ ka? Hon-wa ts'kue-no ue ni arimas´.	Kodomo-wa doko ni imas´ ka? Kodomo-wa ki-no sh'ta ni imas´.

Isu-no ushiro ni nani-ga arimas´ ka? Isu-no ushiro ni tansu-ga arimas´.	Ie-no soba ni dare-ga imas´ ka? Ie-no soba ni otoko-no hito-ga imas´.

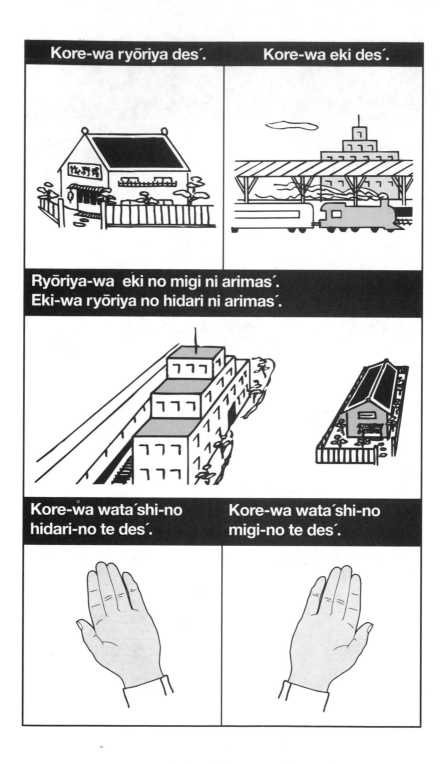

SPEECH PATTERN 13:

A. Ie ni wa denwa-ga arimasen.
There is no telephone in the house.

B. Otoko no ko-wa uchi ni imasen.
The boy is not at home.

EXAMPLES

1. **Suihei-wa ryōriya ni(wa) imasen.**
   The sailors are not in the restaurant.

2. **Otōsan-wa niwa ni(wa) imasen.**
   Father is not in the garden.

3. **Okāsan-wa ki no sh´ta ni(wa) imasen.**
   Mother is not under the tree.

4. **Saifu no naka ni(wa) okane-ga arimasen.**
   There is no money in the purse.

5. **Kono hako no naka ni(wa) kitte-ga arimasen.**
   There is no stamp in this box.

6. **Kono gakkō ni(wa) anata-no shashin-ga arimasen.**
   There is no photograph of you in this school.

NOTES

1. The negative form of *arimas´* is *arimasen*. The negative forms of *imas´* and *orimas´* are *imasen* and *orimasen*, respectively (Speech Pattern 13 A & B).

2. Note that *arimasen* which means "not to be" or "not to exist" is not preceded by *dewa* as was the first form studied (Speech Pattern 13A).

VOCABULARY

denwa .... *telephone*	*otōsan* .... *father*
fūtō .... *envelope*	*shashin* .... *photograph*
kitte ....*postage stamp*	*ts´tsumi (tsutsumi)* ... *package; bundle*
okane .... *money*	*uchi* .... *home*
okāsan .... *mother*	*uma* .... *horse*

EXERCISES

1. Make ten questions using ***doko ni*** with answers in Japanese, for example:

Q: Ts´tsumi-wa doko ni arimas´ ka?
Where is the package?

A: Ts´tsumi-wa tēburu no sh´ta ni arimas´.
The package is under the table.

2. Make ten questions referring to place or existence which require negative answers. Answer each question in Japanese, for example:

Q: Tanaka-san-wa uchi ni imas´ ka?
Is Mr. Tanaka home?

A: Iie, Tanaka-san-wa uchi ni imasen
No, Mr. Tanaka is not home.

Ts´kue-no ue ni hon-ga arimas´ ka?
Iie, ts´kue-no ue ni hon-wa arimasen.
Ts´kue-no ue ni denwa-ga arimas´.

Heya-ni heitai-ga imas´ ka?
Iie, heya-ni heitai-wa imasen.
Heya-ni suihei-ga imas´.

Denwa

Ts'kue

Heya

Suihei

Tēburu-no mae ni kaban-ga arimas´ ka?
Iie, tēburu-no mae ni kaban-wa arimasen.
Tēburu-no mae ni ts´tsumi-ga arimas´.

Shindai-ni akambo-ga imas´ ka?
Iie, shindai-ni akambo-wa imasen.

Ts´tsumi

Michi-ni jidōsha-ga arimas´ ka?
Iie, michi-ni jidōsha-wa arimasen.
Michi-ni jitensha-ga arimasu´.

Michi-ni inu-ga imas´ka?
Iie, michi-ni inu-wa imasen.
Michi-ni uma-ga imas´.

Jitensha

Michi

Uma

Michi

LESSON 13

Hako no naka ni okane to kitte-ga arimas´.
There are money and stamps in the box.

EXAMPLES

1. **Koko-ni koppu to sara-ga arimas.**
   Here are a glass and a dish.

2. **Ringo to momo-wa tēburu no ue ni arimas´.**
   Apples and peaches are on the table.

3. **Ie no mae ni wa jidōsha to jitensha-ga arimas´.**
   In front of the house are a car and a bicycle.

4. **Otōsan to okāsan-wa uchi ni imasen.**
   The father and mother are not home.

5. **Otoko no ko to onna no ko-ga niwa ni imas´.**
   A boy and a girl are in the garden.

6. **Sensei to isha wa eki no soba ni imas´.**
   The teacher and the doctor are near the station.

NOTES

The particle *to* between two names of persons, places, or things (nouns) means "and." Three or even more names of persons, places, or things can be connected in a series by putting *to* after each one except the last. The last is followed by whatever particle the sentence requires—*wa, ga, ni,* etc. (Speech Pattern 14). *To* joins only names of persons, places, or things; it is not used to join any other elements in the sentence.

VOCABULARY

bata .... butter	*ringo* .... apple
fune .... ship; boat	*sara* .... dish; plate
hikōki .... airplane	*shats´ (shatsu)* .... shirt
kagi .... key	*to* .... and (between two nouns)
koppu .... glass (drinking)	*todana* ... cupboard; clothes closet
momo .... peach	*tokei* .... watch; clock
pan .... bread	*zubon* .... trousers

EXERCISES

Express in Japanese:

1. **Bread and butter are on the stand.**

2. **Shirts and pants are in the closet.**

3. **My shoes and hat are in that room.**

4. **The fountain pen and pencil are behind the book.**

5. **Near the house are a man and a woman.**

6. **The ceiling and walls are green.**

Otoko no ko to onna no ko-wa ki no hidari ni imas´.

Isu to dai-wa todana no migi ni arimas´.

Kagi to Tokei

Ringo to Momo

Fune to Hikoki

Pan to Bata

Koppu to Sara

Shats´ to Zubon

SPEECH PATTERN 15:

Wata´shi-wa arakimas´.
I walk. **OR** *I will walk.*

SPEECH PATTERN 16:

Wata´shi-wa arakimasen.
I don't walk. **OR** *I will not walk.*

EXAMPLES

1. **Ano hito-wa ikimas´.**
   He goes. **OR** *He will go.*

2. **Inu-wa tabemas´.**
   The dog eats. **OR** *The dog will eat.*

3. **Wata´shi-wa kakimasen.**
   I don't write. **OR** *I will not write.*

4. **Tomodachi-ga hanashimas´.**
   A friend speaks. **OR** *A friend will speak.*

5. **Otoko no hito-wa yomimasen.**
   The man doesn't read. **OR** *The man will not read.*

6. **Junsa-wa kimasen.**
   The policeman doesn't come.
   OR
   The policeman will not come.

NOTES

The affirmative of the verb for present or definite future action is the base of the verb plus *mas´ (masu)* (Speech Pattern 15). The negative form is the base plus *masen* (Speech Pattern 16).

VOCABULARY

ash´ta (ashita) ... *tomorrow*	***kyō*** .... *today*
hanasu (hanashi) ... *to speak; to talk*	***nomu (nomi)*** .... *to drink*
iku (iki); yuku (yuki) .... *to go*	***taberu (tabe)*** .... *to eat*
kaku (kaki) .... *to write; to draw (pictures)*	***tomodachi*** .... *friend*
kuru (ki) .... *to come*	***yomu (yomi)*** ..... *to read; to peruse*

EXERCISES

Make a series of questions and answers in Japanese using the verbs in the vocabulary, for example:

Q: Dare-ga kimas´ ka?
Who will come?

A: Wata´shi-ga kimas´.
I will come.

Q: Anata-wa ikimas´ ka?
Are you going?

A: Iie, ikimasen.
No, I am not going.

Statue of Buddha

Shinto temple

LESSON 15

Wata´shi-wa arukimash´ta.
I walked.

EXAMPLES

1. **Ano hito-wa kinō kimash´ta.**
   He or she (that person) came yesterday.

2. **Kodomo-wa wasuremash´ta.**
   The child forgot.

3. **Jochū-wa sakuban ikimash´ta.**
   The maid went last night.

4. **Wata´shi-wa kesa ts´kimash´ta.**
   I arrived this morning.

5. **Kono ko-wa kesa hajimete arukimash´ta.**
   This child walked this morning for the first time.

6. **Itsu anata wa yomimash´ta ka?**
   When did you read it?

NOTES

1. The affirmative of the verb for action in the past (past tense) is the base plus *mash'ta (mashita)* (Speech Pattern 17). The past tense of *des´* is *desh'ta*.

2. In Japanese, parts of sentences too obvious to be mentioned are left out particularly in conversation, provided there is no danger of being misunderstood (Example 6).

3. Whenever you agree with the person who spoke to you, your answer can be simply *Hai, sō-des´* (*"Yes, it is so"*). Whenever you disagree with the person who spoke to you, your answer can be simply *Iie, so dewa arimasen* ("No, it is not so").

VOCABULARY

baketsu .... *bucket*	*noren* .... *shop curtain*
desh'ta (deshita) .. *was; were*	*ozen* .... *low table for eating*
geta .... *wooden clogs*	*sakuban* .... *last evening*
hajimete ... *for the first time*	*sensu* .... *folding fan*
hibachi ..... *charcoal heater*	*sō* .... *so*
itsu .... *when*	*tsuzumi* .... *hand drum*
kinō .... *yesterday*	*uchiwa* ...... *non-folding fan*
nagagutsu .... *long boots*	*zōri* .... *sandals*
nani (nan) .... *what?*	*ts'ku (tsuku)* .... *to arrive*

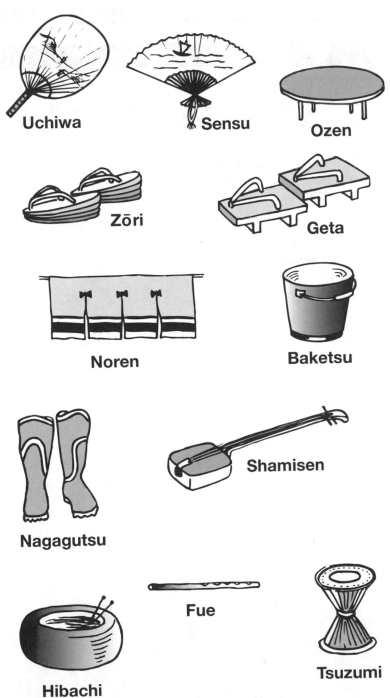

Uchiwa

Sensu

Ozen

Zōri

Geta

Noren

Baketsu

Nagagutsu

Shamisen

Fue

Hibachi

Tsuzumi

EXERCISES

1. Make a series of questions and answers in Japanese expressing time when something was done in the past, for example:

Q: Itsu anata-wa kimash´ta ka?
When did you come?

A: Kinō kimash´ta.
(I) came yesterday.

2. Identify the Japanese objects on page 75 by covering the names and answering in Japanese the question: ***Kore-wa nan des´ ka?*** *("What is this?").*

LESSON **16**

SPEECH PATTERN 18:

Wata´shi-wa sakuban tegami o kakimash´ta.
I wrote a letter last night.

EXAMPLES

1. **Wata´shi-wa kesa shimbun o yomimash´ta.**
   I read the newspaper this morning.

2. **Wata´shi-wa mado-o akemash´ta.**
   I opened the window.

3. **Wata´shi-wa kotoba-o wasuremasen desh´ta.**
   I didn't forget that word.

4. **Anata-wa Eigo-o hanashimas´ ka?**
   Do you speak English?

5. **Wata´shi-wa to-o shimemas´.**
   I will shut the door.

6. **Anata-wa nani-o mimash´ta ka?**
   What did you see?

NOTES

The noun before the particle *o* names the thing upon which the action of the verb is directed or the thing that is acted upon (the direct object). Note that it is placed before the verb.

VOCABULARY

akeru (ake) .... *to open*   *shimeru (shime)* ... *to close*

kau (kai) .... *to buy*   *tegami* .... *letter*

kotoba .... *word*   *wasureru (wasure)* .. *to forget*

miru (mi) .... *to see*

EXERCISES

Express the following questions in Japanese and answer, using as many different nouns as possible.

1. **What did you buy yesterday?**

2. **What are you going to read?**

3. **What do you see?**

SPEECH PATTERN 19:

Wata´shi-wa arakimasen desh´ta.
I didn't walk.

EXAMPLES

1. **Sensei-wa isogimasen desh´ta.**
   The teacher didn't hurry.

2. **Wata´shi-wa kaimasen desh´ta.**
   I didn't buy it.

3. **Seito-wa machigaemasen desh´ta.**
   The student did not make a mistake.

4. **Ano ko-wa shirimasen desh´ta.**
   That child (over there) didn't know.

5. **Wata´shi-wa wasuremasen desh´ta.**
   I did not forget it.

6. **Anata-wa irimasen desh´ta ka?**
   Didn't you need it?

NOTES

The negative form of the verb for action in the past (past tense) is the base plus ***masen desh´ta*** (Speech Pattern 19). The negative form of the past tense of ***des´*** is ***de (wa) arimasen desh´ta***.

VOCABULARY

iru (iri) .... *to need*

isogu (isogi) .... *to hurry; to rush*

machigau (machigae) ... *to make a mistake*

wakaru (wakari) .... *to understand*

EXERCISES

Make a series of questions in Japanese regarding action in the past and answer each of them in the negative, for example:

Q: Anata-wa wakarimash´ta ka?
Did you understand?

A: Wakarimasen desh´ta.
I did not understand.

REVIEW LESSON

A. Review all words indicating the place where a person or thing is to be found or exists. Make a sentence in Japanese illustrating each one.

B. Review all forms of the verbs you have studied. Make a sentence illustrating each form.

VOCABULARY

ago	chin	*kabin*	high vase
ashi	leg; foot	*kakemono*	hanging scroll
ashikubi	ankle	*kami no ke*	hair (on the head)
atama	head		
fusuma	heavy paper door	*kao*	face
ha	tooth	*karada*	body
hana	nose	*kabi*	neck
hara	stomach; abdomen	*kuchi*	mouth
hitai	forehead	*kuchibiru*	lips
hoho	cheek	*me*	eye

VOCABULARY *(cont'd)*

mimi .... *ear*	*tatami* ..... *reed mat; matted floor*
mune .... *chest; breast*	*tekubi* .... *wrist*
okimono .... *ornament*	*tokonoma* .... *alcove*
shōji .... *light paper door*	*ude* .... *arm*
tabako-bon.... *tobacco tray*	*zabuton* .... *cushion*
tana .... *shelf*	

EXERCISES

1. Express in Japanese answers regarding the identity of parts of the body illustrated on page 84, for example:

Q: Kore-wa nan des´ka?
What is this?

A: Sore-wa mimi des´.
That is an ear.

2. Express in Japanese the location of things in the illustration on page 85, for example:

Zabuton-wa tēburu no mae ni arimas´.
A cushion is in front of the table.

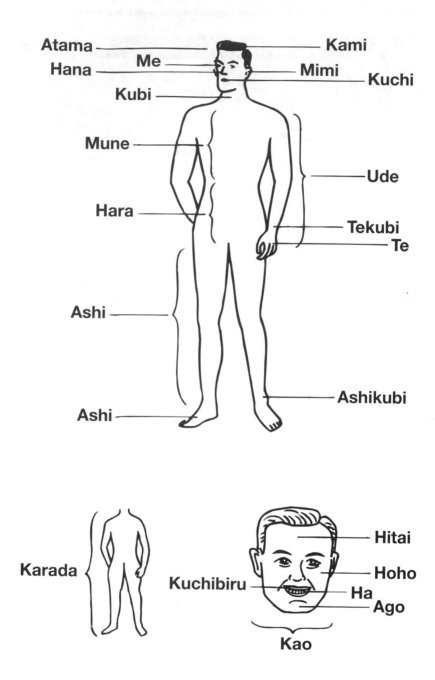

Atama — Kami
Me
Hana — Mimi
Kuchi
Kubi

Mune

Ude

Hara

Tekubi
Te

Ashi

Ashikubi

Ashi

Karada

Hitai

Kuchibiru — Hoho
Ha
Ago

Kao

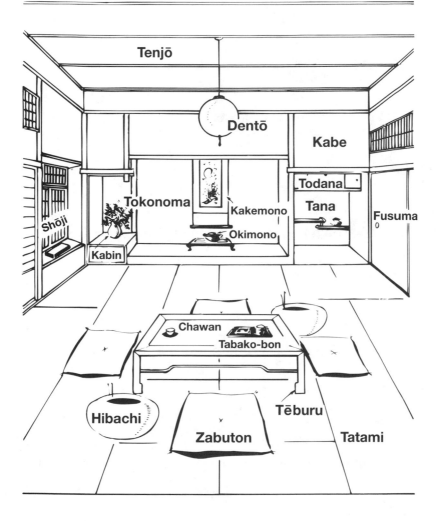

3. Express in Japanese:

1.   The envelope is not on the shelf.

2.   The horse is in the garden.

3.   This watch and fountain pen are not expensive.

4.   He did not buy the apples and peaches here.

5.   That was my teacher.

6. Your father drew this picture.

7. I am going to walk.

8. The Japanese student did not need the book.

9. The American did not make a mistake.

10. Those spectacles on the desk were mine.

4. In the following sentences, the particles are omitted. Fill in each blank with the correct particle. Choose one of these: *wa, ga, na, ni, no, o, ka, san, to*.

a.   Hon-_____doko-_____arimas´_____?

b.   Ts'kue_____ue_____nani_____arimas´_____?

c.   Tanaka-_____Yamamoto-_____arukimasen desh´ta.

d.   Otoko_____ko_____pan_____bata_____tabemash´ta.

e.   Ano hito-_____Nihon_____kotoba_____wasuremash´ta.

f.   Kono sensu_____dare_____des´_____?

g.   Anata_____tomodachi_____Eikokujin des´_____, Beikokujin des´_____?

h.   Sensei_____ie_____naka_____kirei_____kakemono _____arimas´.

SPEECH PATTERN REVIEW

The pictures under **REVIEW A** on page 90 review the use of the particles *no* and *na* between two consecutive nouns or between a quasi-adjective and consecutive noun when the first is intended to identify or modify the second (Lesson 6).

NOTE:

a. That *no* is used only between two nouns and usually only when the first noun is concrete.

b. That *na* is used between a quasi-adjective and a consecutive noun, or between two nouns usually only when the first noun is abstract.

c. That no particle is used when the identifying noun follows the noun it identifies.

d. That no particle is used between a true adjective and a consecutive noun.

The picture under **REVIEW B** on page 91 and questions following review speech patterns which express relative positions (Lessons 10 through 18).

These are the most troublesome constructions taught in Lessons 1 through 18. Students should master them before proceeding to the next lesson. Answers are on pages 198-201.

REVIEW A

1

a. Ano ko wa Amerikajin no otoko no ko desu ka?

b. Ano otoko no ko Amerikajin desu ka?

2

a. Kore wa hen na tori desu ka?

b. Kono tori wa hen desu ka?

3

a. Watakushi no okane wa kin desu ka?

b. Watakushi no wa kin no okane desu ka?

4

a. Ano kirei na onna no hito wa gakkō no sensei desu ka?

b. Ano onna no hito wa kirei desu ka?

5

a. Kono hito wa jōbu desu ka?

b. Kono hito wa jōbu na hito desu ka?

6

Kesa no tenki wa yoi desu ka?

7

a. Kore wa kiiroi dentō dewa arimasen ka?

b. Kono dentō wa kiiroi desu ka?

8

Are ga machi no keisatsusho desu ka?

9

a. Kyō wa atatakai hi dewa arimasen ka?

b. Kyō wa atatakai desu ka?

1. Kono e ni tēburu ga arimasu ka tsukue ga arimasu ka?

2. Isu wa tsukue no mae ni arimasu ka ushiro ni arimasu ka?

3. Tsukue no shita ni nani ga imasu ka?

4. Yuka wa isu no ue ni arimasu ka shita ni arimasu ka?

5. Mado wa tsukue no mae ni arimasu ka?

6. Tsukue no ue ni nani ga arimasu ka?

7. Dare ga sono tegami o kakimashita ka?

8. Jōnzu san wa doko ni imasu ka?

9. Sara no naka ni nani ga arimasu ka?

10. Doko ni dentō ga arimasu ka?

11. Isu to kabe no aida ni nani ga arimasu ka?

12. Sumisu san wa kono heya ni imasu ka?

13. Denwa wa tsukue no ue ni arimasu ka?

14. Tegami to sara wa yuka no ue ni arimasu ka?

15. Mado wa tsukue no soba ni arimasu ka?

Answers for Lesson 18 appear on page 198

LESSON 19

SPEECH PATTERN 20:

Tomodachi ni tegami a kakimashita.
I wrote a letter to my friend.

SPEECH PATTERN 21:

Tōkyō e ikimasu ka?
Are you going to Tokyo?

EXAMPLES

1. **Tanaka san wa heitai ni Nihongo o oshiemashita.**
   Mr. Tanaka taught Japanese to the soldiers.

2. **Kinō watakushi wa Tanaka san ni mannenhitsu o kashimashita.**
   Yesterday I lent my fountain pen to Mr. Tanaka.

3. **Heitai wa kodomo ni okashi o agemashita.**
   The soldier gave some cakes to the children.

4. **Watakushi wa isha ni jidōsha o urimashita.**
   I sold my automobile to the doctor.

5. **Doko e ikimasu ka?**
    Where are you going?

6. **Watakushi wa Tōkyō e kimashita.**
    I came to Tokyo.

VOCABULARY

kasu (kashi-) .... *lend*	*chichi* .... *father (the speaker's)*
okuru (okuri-) .... *send*	*kanai* .. *wife (the speaker's)*
ageru (age-) .... *give (to somebody except the speaker)*	*okashi* .... *cake*
oshieru (oshie-) .... *teach*	*-tachi* .... *plural suffix for persons*
uru (uri-) .... *sell*	*e* .... *to, toward*
haha .... *mother (the speaker's)*	*ni* ..... *particle indicating an indirect object*

NOTES

The particle *ni* has already been introduced as denoting the place where a thing is to be found or exists. It has been shown used in such patterns as *hako no naka ni, tēburu no ue ni, tsukue no ushiro ni, doko ni,* etc. The particle *ni* is also placed after the noun that names the person or thing that receives the indirect act of the verb (Speech Pattern 20). Note that *ni* follows the noun that is the indirect object as *o* follows the noun that is the direct object. The particle *e* is used to denote a direction. Meaning "to" or "toward," it follows the noun to which a movement is directed (Speech Pattern 21).

EXERCISES

Express in Japanese:

1. **I wrote a letter this morning.**

2. **To whom did you send it?**

3. **I sent it to my father.**

4. **Where is your father?**

5. **He is in Osaka. He is coming to Tokyo tomorrow.**

6. My father sold that house (over there) to Mr. Tanaka.

7. Is your mother in Osaka?

8. No, my mother is not in Osaka.

9. She came to Tokyo yesterday.

10. My mother teaches English to my wife.

Answers for Lesson 19
appear on page 202

LESSON 20

SPEECH PATTERN 22:

Isu ga futatsu arimasu.
There are two chairs.

SPEECH PATTERN 23:

Watakushi wa hako o yottsu kaimashita.
I bought four boxes.

EXAMPLES

1. **Bōshi ga itsutsu arimasu. (Itsutsu no bōshi ga arimasu.)**
   There are five hats.

2. **Isu wa ikutsu arimasu ka?**
   How many chairs are there?

3. **Yottsu arimasu.**
   There are four.

4. **Tsukue no ue ni ringo ga mittsu arimasu. (Tsukue no ue ni mittsu no ringo ga arimasu.)**
   Three apples are on the desk.

5. **Okashi o ikutsu tomodachi ni agemashita ka?**
   How many cakes did you give your friend?

6. **(Watakushi wa) Okashi o nanatsu agemashita.**
   I gave seven cakes.

VOCABULARY

hitotsu	one	*yattsu*	eight
futatsu	two	*kokonotsu*	nine
mittsu	three	*tō*	ten
yottsu	four	*daidokoro*	kitchen
itsutsu	five	*saji*	spoon
muttsu	six	*ikutsu*	how many
nanatsu	seven		

NOTES

In Japanese there are *two sets of numbers from one to ten.* The set given in the vocabulary for this lesson stops at ten; the other set goes on above ten. Note that the numbers of this first set are nouns; therefore, when they are used as adjectives to modify nouns they must be followed by the particle *no* as in the case of quasi-adjectives. For example:

1. **Futatsu no me**
   2 eyes

2. **Mittsu no isu**
   3 chairs

3. **Yottsu no hako**
    4 boxes

But when these numbers refer to a noun that is the subject or direct object, the most common method is that used in the Speech Pattern sentences for this lesson. Note that the number follows the particle that follows the subject or object noun. The Speech Pattern sentences, of course, could be expressed:

a. *Futatsu no isu ga arimasu.*

b. *Watakushi wa yottsu no hako o kaimashita.*

EXERCISES

Express in Japanese:

1. **How many apples are there on the table?**

2. **There are nine apples.**

3. **Did you give an apple to that child?**

4. **I did not give an apple.**

5. **I am going to give five cakes now.**

6. How many pencils are there in the box now?

7. There are ten. There are five on the desk.

8. Tomorrow I shall give four pencils and six notebooks to my Japanese friend.

9. That is good. Now I will give you three of these apples.

10. Thank you very much. Will you come to my house to-day?

11. I am sorry. Today I go to school.

12. Oh, I see. I have forgotten. Will you come to my house tomorrow?

13. Yes. Thank you very much.

Answers for Lesson 20 appear on page 203

LESSON 21

Watakushi wa ashita ikimashō.
I shall (probably) go tomorrow.

Kore wa anata no hon deshō.
This is (probably) your book.

Ima tabemashō.
Let us eat now.

EXAMPLES

1. **Asatte kono hon o yomimashō.**
   The day after tomorrow I shall (probably) read this book.

2. **Ashita wa tabun samui deshō.**
   Tomorrow it will probably be cold.

3. **Ano hito wa Amerikajin deshō.**
   That person is an American, I suppose.

4. **Sore wa empitsu deshō ka?**
   I wonder, isn't that a pencil?

5. **Watakushi ga akemashō ka?**
   Do you want me to open it? (Shall I open it?)

6. **Ima nani o shimashō ka?**
   What shall we do now?

NOTES

The verb form ***deshō*** and the ending ***-mashō*** express conditions less positive or less certain than do ***desu*** and ***-masu***. They are used to express an inducement or a desire for confirmation of a fact. Sometimes they are used for the future tense, but they are more appropriate for expressing a future idea than are ***desu*** and ***-masu*** only in so far as the future, by nature, is less certain than the present.

VOCABULARY

deshō .... *form of* **desu** *denoting probability or conjecture*

-masho .... *verb ending denoting probability or conjecture*

suru (shi-) .... *do*

asatte .... *the day after tomorrow*

issho ni .... *together*

to .... *with (in or into company of)*

tabun .... *probably*

komban .... *tonight*

gohan .... *cooked rice; a meal*

EXERCISES

Express in Japanese:

1. **When is Mr. Brown coming to Tokyo?**

2. **He will (probably) come the day after tomorrow.**

3. **Mr. Smith will probably come tonight.**

4. **Let us take a meal together with him tomorrow.**

5. **Mr. Tanaka and Mr. Brown will probably come together.**

6. Is that so?

7. Yes, they will probably arrive in the morning.

8. Then probably the next day Mr. Tanaka, together with Mr. Brown, will go to Tokyo.

9. I think so. When shall we eat?

10. Let us eat early in the evening.

Answers for Lesson 21
appear on page 204

SPEECH PATTERN 25A:

Jidōsha de ikimashita.
I went by automobile.

SPEECH PATTERN 25B:

Sore o ki de tsukurimashita.
I made it with wood.

SPEECH PATTERN 25C:

Kono gakkō de Nippongo o naraimasu.
I learn Japanese at this school.

EXAMPLES

1. **Empitsu de tegami o kakimashita.**
   I wrote the letter with a pencil.

2. **Chichi to denwa de hanashimashita.**
   I talked with my father by phone.

3. **Doko de Furansugo o naraimashita ka?**
   Where did you learn French?

4. **Kono heya de Nippongo o hanashimashō.**
   Let us speak Japanese in this room.

5. **Anata wa jimusho de hatarakimasu ka?**
   Do you work in an office?

6. **Jimusho de (wa) hatarakimasen. Honya de hatarakimasu.**
   I do not work in an office. I work at a bookstore.

NOTES

De is placed after the word that denotes the means by which something is done (Speech Pattern 25A), the material with which something is made (Speech Pattern 25B), or the location where an action or process takes place (Speech Pattern 25C).

VOCABULARY

tsukuru (tsukuri-) .... *make*

narau (narai-) .... *learn*

hataraku (hataraki-) ... *work*

kiku (kiki-) .... *hear*

jimusho .... *office*

honya .... *bookstore*

bangohan .... *dinner (evening meal)*

ongaku .... *music*

rajio .... *radio*

sorekara ... *then, afterwards*

EXERCISES

Express in Japanese:

1. I went to Kamakura yesterday.

2. Did you go by electric train?

3. No, I went by car.

4. What did you see at Kamakura?

5. I saw the Great Buddha.

6. Where did you eat dinner?

7. I ate dinner at home.

8. Then, I heard music on the radio.

9. Afterwards I wrote a letter to my mother with my new fountain pen.

10. Then I went to a movie with my friend.

Answers for Lesson 22
appear on page 205

SPEECH PATTERN 26A:

Empitsu o yonhon kaimashita.
I bought four pencils.

SPEECH PATTERN 26B:

Otoko no hito ga gonin kimashita.
Five men came.

SPEECH PATTERN 26C:

Kyō kono gohon no empitsu o kaimashita.
I bought these five pencils today.

EXAMPLES

1. **Ie no mae ni ki ga ikuhon arimasu ka?**
   How many trees are in front of the house?

2. **Ie no mae ni ki ga nijū-nihon arimasu.**
   In front of the house there are twenty-two trees.

3. **Kono heya ni hito ga nannin imasu ka?**
   How many people are in this room?

4. **Sono hako no naka ni sara ga ikumai arimasu ka?**
    How many plates are in that box?

5. **Sono rokumai no sara wa kirei desu.**
    Those six plates are clean.

6. **Sono gakkō de sanjū-shichinin no heitai ga Nippongo o naraimashita.**
    Thirty-seven soldiers studied Japanese in that school.

VOCABULARY

ichi	one	*jū*	ten
ni	two	*jūichi*	eleven
san	three	*jūni*	twelve
shi (or yon)	four	*jūsan*	thirteen (etc.)
go	five	*nijū*	twenty
roku	six	*nijū-ichi*	twenty-one
shichi (or nana)	seven	*nijū-ni*	twenty-two (etc.)
hachi	eight	*sanjū*	thirty
ku (or kyū)	nine	*shijū (or yonjū)*	forty (etc.)
hyaku	one hundred	*roppyaku*	six hundred
nihyaku	two hundred	*nanahyaku*	seven hundred
sambyaku	three hundred	*happyaku*	eight hundred
yonhyaku	four hundred	*kyūhyaku*	nine hundred
gohyaku	five hundred		

VOCABULARY *(cont'd)*

minna .... *all*

mai .... *word used in counting flat objects (sheets of paper, boards,cloth, dishes, coins, etc.)*

hon .... *word used in counting long objects (trees, bottles, sticks, legs, ciga-rettes, etc.)*

hitori .... *one person*

futari .... *two people*

nin .... *word used in counting more than two human beings*

nan- or *iku-* .... *prefix for mai, hon, nin, etc., meaning "how many"*

NOTES

This is the second system of numerals in Japanese. It is the system that must be used for all counting above ten.

As in English we use such expressions as "so many pieces of chalk" or "so many head of cattle," so the Japanese use expressions corresponding to "pieces" and "head" in the counting of many things. Besides those taken up in this lesson, there are many more.

Note the fact that special words are used for referring to one or two human beings; the word *nin* is used for referring to three or more human beings.

Usually with this second system of numerals, the number and its numerative follow the noun to which they refer (see Speech Patterns 26A and B). But if one speaks of a certain group, as "those four men are coming," the number reference precedes the noun: ***Sono yonin no hito ga kimasu*** (see Speech Pattern 26C).

Euphonic changes. The Japanese expressions for "three hundred," "six hundred," and "eight hundred" depart from the regular pattern of the number plus the word *hyaku*. These departures represent phonetic changes that have eliminated certain awkward speech sound combinations. In English, when we say "an apple" instead of "a apple," we exercise the same kind of sound change.

EXERCISES

Express in Japanese:

1. How many houses are there in this town?

2. There are three hundred forty-two houses.

3. How many people are there?

4. There are one thousand five hundred people in this town.

5. How many sheets of paper are in the box?

6. Six sheets.

7. Are there pencils in the box?

8. Yes, there are five pencils in the box.

9. How many red pencils are in the box?

10. Three.

11. There are no yellow pencils in the box, are there?

12. No, there are none.

Answers for Lesson 23
appear on page 206

Local restaurant

Buddha

SPEECH PATTERN 27A:

Anata wa nanji ni bangohan o tabemasu ka?
What time do you eat dinner?

SPEECH PATTERN 27B:

Rokuji jūgofun ni.
At six-fifteen.

EXAMPLES

1. **Watakushi wa asagohan o rokuji han ni tabemasu.**
   I eat breakfast at 6:30.

2. **Anata wa itsu kara koko ni imasu ka?**
   How long (since when) have you been here?

3. **Jūji kara.**
   Since ten o'clock.

4. **Ano hito wa koko ni itsu made imasu ka?**
   How long (until when) will he be here?

5. Densha wa hachiji jippun mae ni demasu.
The electric train leaves at ten minutes before eight.

6. Ano hito wa kisha de jūsanji nijū-gofun ni tsukimashita.
He arrived by train at 13:25.

NOTES

The particle *ni* indicates the point of time of an action. In Japan both the A.M. – P.M. and the 24-hour time systems are used. Governmental business and transportation systems use the latter; however, the former system is generally in use elsewhere.

When expressing time *after* the hour in Japanese, the expression for "after" *(sugi)* is usually omitted—as it is in English; but when expressing time *before* the hour, the expression for "before" *(mae)* is always expressed.

The word *fun* is subject to phonetic changes as in Lesson 23 we observed concerning *hyaku*:

ippun .... *one minute*

sampun .... *three minutes*

yompun .... *four minutes*

roppun .... *six minutes*

juppun .... *ten minutes*

VOCABULARY

ji	o'clock	**made**	until, up to, as far as
jikan	time, hour	**kara**	since, from
fun	minute	**gozen**	forenoon, A.M.
byō	second	**gogo**	afternoon, P.M.
mae	before	**densha**	electric train
sugi	after	**asagohan**	breakfast
han	half past	**deru (de-)***	go out, come out, depart

*Note that usually the particle "o" is required after the name of the place from which departure is made when the verb **deru** is used.

EXERCISES

Express in Japanese:

1. **What time did you leave Tokyo station yesterday?**

2. **I left at 10:15 A.M.**

3. **When did you arrive here?**

4. I arrived here at 3:20 P.M.

5. Until when will you be here?

6. I shall (probably) be here until tomorrow.

7. Will you depart tomorrow morning or tomorrow afternoon?

8. I shall be here until noon tomorrow.

9. Will you go by electric train?

10. Yes, on the 1:30 train.

Answers for Lesson 24
appear on page 208

SPEECH PATTERN 28A:

Ashita wa naniyōbi desu ka?
What day of the week is tomorrow?

SPEECH PATTERN 28B:

Doyōbi ni hachiji kara jūniji made hatarakimasu.
On Saturday I work from eight to twelve.

SPEECH PATTERN 28C:

Maiasa rokuji han ni okimasu.
Every morning I get up at six-thirty.

EXAMPLES

1. **Ano hito wa mainichi Mainichi shimbun o yomimasu.**
   Everyday he reads the Mainichi.

2. **Anata wa naniyōbi ni dekakemasu ka?**
   What day of the week will you go out?

3. **Anata wa maiban nanji ni yasumimasu ka?**
   What time do you go to bed every night?

4. **(Watakushi wa) Jūninichi ni Tōkyō e ikimasu.**
   I will go to Tokyo on the 12th.

5. **(Watakushi wa) Ano hi ni Tōkyō e ikimashita.**
   I went to Tokyo on that day.

6. **(Watakushi wa) Tabun tsugi no Suiyōbi ni Ōsaka e kaerimashō.**
   I shall probably return to Osaka next Wednesday.

NOTES

As has already been noted, the Japanese language sometimes requires the use of different words to name the same thing depending upon whether the thing is being named by itself or is being compounded with some other word or words. For example, the word for "day" is *hi*, but "everyday" is *mainichi*; "night," is *yoru*, but "every night" is *maiban*, meaning literally "every evening."

VOCABULARY

dekakeru (dekake-) ... *go out*	*mai-* .... *every (prefix)*
okiru (oki-) .... *get up*	*tsugi* .... *next*
yasumu (yasumi-) ... *to rest, go to bed*	*Nichiyōbi* .... *Sunday*
	Getsuyōbi .... *Monday*
hi .... *day*	*Kayōbi* .... *Tuesday*
-nichi .... *day (in compounds)*	*Suiyōbi* .... *Wednesday*

VOCABULARY *(cont'd)*

Mokuyōbi .... Thursday	*Doyōbi* .... Saturday
Kinyōbi .... Friday	*naniyōbi* .... what day of the week

EXERCISES

Express in Japanese:

1. **What time will you go out tonight?**

2. **I will go out at six o'clock.**

3. **Shall we go to Kamakura next Sunday?**

4. **Let's go there next Saturday afternoon.**

5. Don't you work on Saturday?

6. I don't work every Saturday.

7. How many hours do you work from Monday to Friday?

8. Forty hours.

9. Don't you work every day of the week?

10. No, I rest on Sunday.

Answers for Lesson 25
appear on page 209

LESSON 26

Hachi wa shichi yori ōkii desu.
Eight is larger than seven.

Ichi to ni to san no naka de san ga ichiban ōkii desu.
Of one, two, and three, three is the largest.

EXAMPLES

1. **Anata wa watakushi yori ōkii desu.**
   You are bigger than I.

2. **Kore ga ichiban nagai desu.**
   This is the longest.

3. **Dochira ga motto takai desu ka?**
   Which is more expensive?

4. **Ōkii hō ga motto takai desu.**
   The larger one is more expensive.

5. **Dore ga ichiban yasui kimono desu ka?**
   Which is the cheapest kimono?

6. **Ichigatsu wa ichiban samui tsuki desu.**
   January is the coldest month.

NOTES

Adjectives in Japanese do not have any forms like the *-er* and *-est* forms of English adjectives (bigg*er*, bigg*est*). In a sentence like "This is bigger than that," the word *yori* (than) is used after the second element of the comparison: *Kore wa sore yori okii desu.* To a question like *Ichigatsu to Nigatsu to dochira ga samui desu ka?* (Which is colder, January or February?) the answer is *Ichigatsu no hō ga samui desu* (January is colder), or literally, "January side is cold." If the subject is a true adjective, such as *Ōkii ho ga takai desu* (The big one is more expensive), the particle *no* is omitted. The *-est* meaning, or superlative degree, is expressed simply by the word *ichiban* (see Example 6 above).

VOCABULARY

yori .... *than*	*hō* .... *side, direction*
ichiban ..... *No. 1; the most; sign of the superlative degree*	*motto* .... *more*
	mo .... *also, too*
no naka .... *among*	*Ichigatsu* .... *January*
dochira .... *which (of two)*	*Nigatsu* .... *February*
dore .... *which (of three or more)*	*Sangatsu* .... *March*

VOCABULARY *(cont´d)*

Shigatsu	April	*Kugatsu*	September
Gogatsu	May	*Jūgatsu*	October
Rokugatsu	June	*Jūichigatsu*	November
Shichigatsu	July	*Jūnigatsu*	December
Hachigatsu	August		

EXERCISES

1. When did you go to Kyoto?

2. I went in June.

3. Was it hot in Kyoto? (Was Kyoto hot?)

4. It was not very hot. August will (probably) be hotter.

5. Was Kyoto hotter than Tokyo?

6. Yes, it was (hotter).

7. Did you go to Nara, too?

8. Yes, I went there, too.

9. Which is more beautiful, Tokyo or Kyoto?

10. Kyoto is more beautiful. Kyoto is the most beautiful town
    in Japan.

11. Which is the largest town, Tokyo, Kyoto or Nara?

12. Tokyo is the largest.

Answers for Lesson 26
appear on page 210

LESSON 27

REVIEW LESSON

This lesson is a review designed to determine how well students have learned the basic patterns of expression and how readily they can use them in conversation. The following pictures with captions illustrate all the speech patterns which have been studied from Lesson 1 through Lesson 26. Some of the captions make statements and others ask questions. Of those which make statements, some are true and others are false. Responses should be grammatically complete statements, such as: "Yes, this is a radio," or "No, that is not a steam train, it is an electric train." Answers are on pages 221-224.

1	2	3
Kore wa densha desu.	Kore wa jidōsha desu ka?	Kore wa haizara dewa arimasen.

4	5	6
Kore wa chiisai ie desu.	Kore wa karui desu.	Kono hito wa ojiisan desu.

7	8	9
Kore wa sumisu san no empitsu desu.	Kono hon wa sumisu san no desu.	Kono hito wa Nihon no toko no hito desu.

10	11	12
Kono hito wa jōbu na otoko no hito desu.	Ano fune wa chiisaku wa arimasen.	Ima wa haru desu ka, natsu desu ka?

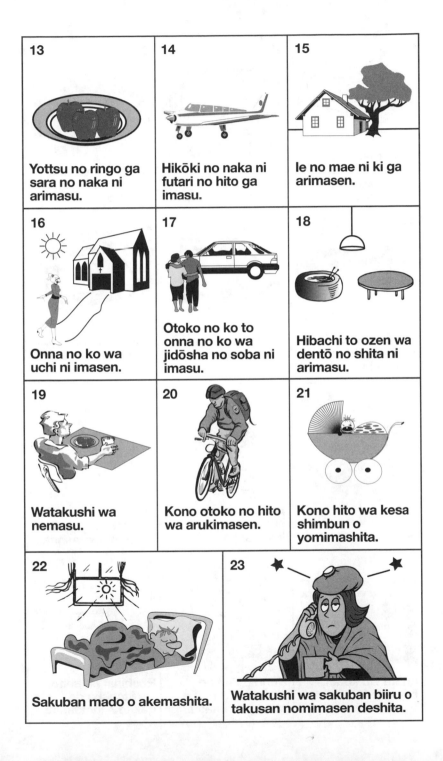

13 Yottsu no ringo ga sara no naka ni arimasu.

14 Hikōki no naka ni futari no hito ga imasu.

15 Ie no mae ni ki ga arimasen.

16 Onna no ko wa uchi ni imasen.

17 Otoko no ko to onna no ko wa jidōsha no soba ni imasu.

18 Hibachi to ozen wa dentō no shita ni arimasu.

19 Watakushi wa nemasu.

20 Kono otoko no hito wa arukimasen.

21 Kono hito wa kesa shimbun o yomimashita.

22 Sakuban mado o akemashita.

23 Watakushi wa sakuban biiru o takusan nomimasen deshita.

24	25	26
Watakushi wa kono tegami o dōe san no okusan ni okurimas.	Kono basu wa atami e ikimasu.	Bōshi ga nanatsu tēburu no ue ni arimasu.

27	28	29
Watakushi wa suika o mittsu kaimashita.	Ashita wa tabun samui hi deshō.	Watakushitachi wa tabun ashita umi e ikimashō.

30	31	32
Ima yasumimashō.	Watakushi wa jidōsha de yama e ikimashita.	Kono bōto wa ki de tsukurimashita.

33	34	35
Anata wa kono heya de furansugo o naraimasu ka?	Kono byōin no mae hi ki ga roppon arimasu.	Hachinin no seito wa jitensha de gakkō e kimashita.

36

Kono yonhon no ki wa byōin no ushiro ni arimasu.

37

Anata wa maiasa nanji ni okimasu ka?

38

Leaves
10:15

Kono kisha wa hiru ni demasu.

39

Anata wa naniyōbi ni yasumimasu ka?

40

Mon Tue Wed Thu
Fri
Sat
Sun

Anata wa mainichi hachiji kara goji made benkyō o shimasu ka?

41

Natsu ni wa maiban yuki ga furimasu.

42

Naniyōbi no ban ni anata wa kyōkai e ikimasu ka?

43

Chiisai onno no ko wa ōkii otoko no ko yori ōkii desu.

44

Migi no empitsu ga ichiban nagai desu.

45

¥1800   ¥3000   ¥5000

Dono Kimono ga ichiban takai desu ka?

46

Dochira ga furui jidōsha desu ka?

SPEECH PATTERN 30A:

Sumisu san wa Nihongo o hanasu koto ga dekimasu.
Mr. Smith can speak Japanese.

SPEECH PATTERN 30B:

Kyō iku koto ga dekimasen.
I cannot go today.

EXAMPLES

1. **Tanaka san wa araku koto ga dekimasen.**
   Mr. Tanaka cannot walk.

2. **(Anata wa) Komban benkyō suru koto ga dekimasu ka?**
   Can you study tonight?

3. **(Anata wa) Nippongo o yomu koto ga dekimasu ka?**
   Can you read Japanese?

4. **(Watakushi wa) Kono mado o akeru koto ga dekimasen.**
   I cannot open this window.

5. **Eigo ga dekimasu ka?**
   Can you (speak) English?

6. **Hai, dekimasu.**
   Yes, I can.

NOTES

The Japanese for all the verbs taken up so far has been given in two forms; for instance, "eat" has been given in Japanese *"taberu (tabe-)."* The form in the parenthesis is the form that is used with the "polite" form of the verb; with **-masu, -masen,** etc. This "polite" form is the only form of the verb that we have been dealing with. The other form, like **taberu**, is sometimes called the "abrupt" form, or the "dictionary" form because this is the form in which the verb is given in the dictionary. This "dictionary" form is really the present tense of the verb, as is also the **-masu** form. So far we have taken up only the **-masu** form because in polite Japanese conversation this form should be used at least once in every sentence.

The shorter form, the dictionary form, however, is necessary for various purposes. One of these purposes is that of expressing the "can do" construction known as the potential form of the verb. (There are other ways of expressing this potential idea in Japanese. But this one is the most simple to learn.)

VOCABULARY

(verb) koto ga dekimasu .... *"can do"* whatever the supplied verb denotes	*(verb) koto ga dekimasen.* ..... *"cannot do"* whatever the supplied verb denotes

EXERCISES

Express in Japanese:

1. **Can you go to Tokyo tomorrow?**

2. **No, I cannot go tomorrow.**

3. **Shall we go on Wednesday?**

4. **I cannot go on Wednesday.**
    I will read this book on that day.

5. **Can you read a Japanese book?**

6. No, I cannot read Japanese.

7. Can you speak Japanese?

8. I can speak Japanese a little.
    I can also understand a little.

9. Can't you write Japanese?

10. No, I cannot read nor write Japanese.

Answers for Lesson 28
appear on page 211

LESSON 29

SPEECH PATTERN 31:

(Watakushi wa) Hayaku arukimashita.
I walked fast.

SPEECH PATTERN 32:

Ano hito wa Nihongo o kirei ni kakimasu.
He writes Japanese beautifully.

EXAMPLES

1. **Ano hito wa Eigo o yoku hanashimasu.**
   He speaks English well.

2. **(Watakushi wa) Kono ie o renga de hayaku tatemashita.**
   I built this house quickly with bricks.

3. **(Watakushi wa) Kesa hayaku okimashita.**
   I got up early this morning.

4. **Ano hito wa yoku hatarakimasu.**
   He works well.

5. **(Watakushi wa) Kono jibiki o yasuku kaimashita.**
   I bought this dictionary cheaply.

6. **Ano hito wa jōzu ni oshiemasu.**
   He teaches skillfully.

NOTES

In Japanese there are those words, as there are in English, that are primarily used as adverbs (words which modify verbs, adjectives, and adverbs). We have already taken up some of these like *itsumo*, *mata*, *sugu*, and *taihen*. But in Japanese, as in English, adjectives with some alteration may be used as adverbs. In English we can take adjectives like *tight* or *rough* and add *-ly* to them and form adverbs, *tightly* or *roughly*.

In Japanese we can use all the "true adjectives" as adverbs by changing the final *-i* to *-ku*. By this operation an adjective like *hayai* becomes an adverb *hayaku*. (Note that this *-ku* form of the true adjective is the same as the negative adjective we took up in Lesson 7.)

"Quasi-adjectives" like *kirei (na)* and *jōzu (na)* may be used as adverbs by adding the particle *ni*.

VOCABULARY

tateru (tate-)	build	**jibiki**	dictionary
renga	brick	**hayaku**	fast, quick, early *(adverb)*

EXERCISES

Express in Japanese:

1. **I am going to the bookstore early tomorrow morning.**

2. **Is that so? At what time?**

3. **At eight o'clock. I can buy books cheaply there tomorrow.**

4. **Do you read Japanese easily?**

5. **Yes, I can read it well. I cannot write skillfully.**

6. Is the bookstore far?

7. Yes, it is far. But I can go there quickly in my car.

8. Shall we go together?

9. Yes. Let's do that.

10. Then let's go to bed soon.

**Answers for Lesson 29
appear on page 212**

LESSON 30

SPEECH PATTERN 33:

Kono empitsu wa mijikaku narimashita.
This pencil became short.

SPEECH PATTERN 34:

Buraun san wa gunsō ni narimashita.
Brown became a sergeant.

EXAMPLES

1. **Kyōto wa taihen samuku narimashita ka?**
   Did it become very cold in Kyoto? (Did Kyoto become very cold?)

2. **Gunsō wa taii ni narimasen deshita.**
   The sergeant did not become a captain.

3. **Yamamoto san no inu wa taihen ōkiku narimashita.**
   Mr. Yamamoto's dog got very big.

4. **Jidosha wa mō yasuku narimashita.**
   The automobile had already become cheap.

5. **Ano hito wa tōtō yoi hito ni narimashita.**
   He finally became a good man.

6. **Kodomo wa kanari kirei ni narimashita.**
   The child became fairly pretty.

NOTES

The verb *naru (nari-)* means "to become" in such senses as the verbs in the expressions "He became a captain"; "It got expensive"; "The weather turned cold." As in these examples in English, either a noun or an adjective may be used with this "become" verb. In Japanese the same condition applies, with the following forms:

Noun or pronoun PLUS *ni nari-masu*, *-masen*, *-mashita*, *-masen deshita*.

-ku form of true adjective PLUS *nari-masu*, *-masen*, *-mashita*, *-masen deshita*.

VOCABULARY

naru (nari-) .... become, get, turn	*taihen* .... very
	tōtō .... finally
mō .... already	*kanari* .... fairly
gunsō .... sergeant	*taii* .... captain

EXERCISES

Express in Japanese:

1. Will the weather become good tomorrow?

2. I don't think so. The weather is not good in June.

3. Is the weather in Japan not good?

4. In the spring there are warm days and cool days. In March, April, and May there is not much rain. But in June, the weather becomes bad. From June to July there is much rain. In July, the weather becomes very hot.

5. Doesn't Tokyo become very hot in summer?

6. Yes, it becomes very hot. In July and August many people go to the seaside and to the mountains.

7. When does it become cool?

8. In September, the weather again becomes cool.

9. Isn't autumn in Japan very beautiful?

10. Yes, Japan becomes beautiful in the autumn. The trees in the mountains turn red.

11. Does it get cold in winter?

12. Yes, I think so. It becomes very cold in December, January, and February. It also snows very much.

**Answers for Lesson 30
appear on page 213**

LESSON **31**

SPEECH PATTERN 35A:

(Watakushi wa) Bangohan o tabete imasu.
I am eating dinner.

SPEECH PATTERN 35B:

(Watakushi wa) Tegami o kaite imasen deshita.
I was not writing a letter.

SPEECH PATTERN 35C:

Ano hito wa hon o yonde imashita.
He was reading the book.

EXAMPLES

1. **Iie, watakushi wa hako o akete imasen.**
   No, I am not opening the box.

2. **(Anata wa) Ima ie o tatete imasu ka?**
   Are you building a house now?

3. **Fune wa ugoite imasu.**
   The ship is moving.

4. (Watakushi wa) Kono gakkō de Nippongo o
    naratte imasu.
    I am learning Japanese at this school.

5. (Anata wa) Ima nani o nonde imasu ka?
    What are you drinking now?

6. (Anata wa) Doko de hataraite imasu ka?
    Where are you working?

NOTES

The progressive or continuing action verb introduces for this course the *-te* form of the Japanese verb. (See column 3 on page 185.) This form is important to learn because it is used in many common Japanese expressions.

While as in English the progressive form of the verb is formed with a part of the verb "to be," the literal translation of the Japanese *-ing* verb form is quite different from its English translation. The expression *tabete imasu* (am eating) literally translates something like "eat" *(tabe-)*, "and" *(-te)*, "am" *(imasu)*. It all amounts to something like "I eat and continue to eat." The form *imasu*, *imasen*, etc., is used whether the subject is animate or inanimate.

Note: Some of these *-te* forms are not simply the addition of *-te* to the so-called stem. While many verbs like *tabemasu* are simply changed by replacing the *-masu* with *-te*, others, for euphonic reasons, are subject to more of a change. For instance, if *yomimasu* received the same simple treatment as does *tabemasu*, it would become *yomte*, obviously a very awkward sound. Even *yomde* is vocally difficult; the phonetic solution,

therefore, is *yonde*. Also, for *arukimasu* the form *arukte* phonetically is almost impossible; *aruite* is the solution. The patterns of these changes are not many; it is a good idea to memorize them. (See column 3 on page 185.)

VOCABULARY

-te form of verb PLUS imasu .... *am doing, is doing, are doing whatever the supplied verb stem denotes.*

-te form of verb PLUS imasen .... *am not doing, is not doing, are not doing whatever the supplied verb stem denotes.*

-te form of verb PLUS imashita .... *was doing, were doing whatever the supplied verb stem denotes.*

-te form of verb PLUS imasen deshita .... *was not doing, were not doing whatever the supplied verb stem denotes.*

ugoku (ugoki-, ugoite) ... *move*

EXERCISES

Express in Japanese:

1. **What are you doing?**

2. **I am writing a letter to my father.**

3. Where is your father?

4. He is working in Tokyo.

5. How long (from when) has he been working in Tokyo?

6. He was working in Yokohama until September. Then he went to Tokyo.

7. Can you go to Tokyo with me the day after tomorrow?

8. No, I cannot go. I am teaching every day in a Japanese school.

9. Oh, I see. Are you going to Tokyo soon?

10. No, I will be in Kyoto until autumn.

11. Then where are you going?

12. I am probably going to school in America.

Answers for Lesson 31
appear on page 215

Wish tree-heian, Jingu shrine

Rice planting

LESSON 32

SPEECH PATTERN 36A:

Ano hito wa gakkō e aruite kimashita.
He came to school on foot.

SPEECH PATTERN 36B:

Anata wa hon o motte kimasu ka?
Are you bringing the book?

SPEECH PATTERN 37:

Ano hito wo okashi o katte tabemashita.
He bought cakes and ate them.

EXAMPLES

1. **Ano hito wa okashi o kodomo ni motte ikimasen.**
   He is not taking the cakes to the children.

2. **Anata no uchi e aruite ikimashō.**
   Let's go to your house on foot. (Let's walk to your house.)

3. **Kamakura e shashinki o motte ikimashō.**
   Let's take a camera to Kamakura.

4. **Otōto wa ani ni kasa o motte kimashita.**
   My younger brother brought an umbrella to my older brother.

5. **Niku o katte koko e motte kimashita.**
   I bought meat and brought it here.

6. **Ane wa mannenhitsu o katte imōto ni agemashita.**
   My older sister bought a fountain pen and gave it to my younger sister.

NOTES

The *-te* form of the verb in Japanese can be used in succession with other verbs to render various meanings. If one remembers that the *-te* (or *-de*) in this form carries the idea of "and," the combination of the verbs can be translated with the idea of the English meaning. The expression ***motte kimasu***, for instance, by analysis gives us "hold (or have) and come"; it is not difficult, therefore, to see how this corresponds to the English meaning of "bring." We see the same correspondence between ***motte ikimasu*** literally meaning "hold (or have) and go," and the English "take."

VOCABULARY

motsu (mochi-, motte) ... *hold or have*

aruku (aruki-, aruite) ... *walk*

niku .... *meat*

ane (nēsan*) ... *older sister*

imōto* .... *younger sister*

VOCABULARY *(cont'd)*

ani (niisan*) .... *older*   *otōto* .... *younger brother*
brother

* The honorific *o* is prefixed to these words of family
relationship when they refer to members of the family of the
person being addressed. The honorific should also be used
when these words refer to the person being addressed. Note
that *ane*, *ani*, *chichi*, and *haha* are used only when speaking about one's own older sister, older brother, father, or
mother. They are never used when speaking to one's own or
about some other person's sister, brother, father, or mother
and, therefore, are never prefixed with the honorific *o*.

EXERCISES

Express in Japanese:

1.   **Are you going to take your camera to Kamakura?**

2.   **No, I am not taking mine. Can you bring yours?**

3.   **Yes, I will bring mine. Are you going to take your lunch?**

4. No, I will buy lunch at a restaurant in Kamakura.

5. Are you going by car or on foot?

6. I shall take my car (go in my car).

7. How many people will go with you?

8. Four people will go—you, my younger sister, my older brother, and my friend.

Answers for Lesson 32
appear on page 216

LESSON 33

SPEECH PATTERN 38A:

(Moshi) Ame ga furu nara, (watakushi wa) ikimasen.
If it rains, I will not go.

SPEECH PATTERN 38B:

(Moshi) Yasui nara, (watakushi wa) kaimasu.
If (it is) cheap, I will buy (it).

SPEECH PATTERN 39:

Ame ga furu to, (watakushi wa) uchi ni imasu.
Whenever it rains, I stay at home.

EXAMPLES

1. **Ashita yuki ga furu nara, (anata wa) nani o shimasu ka?**
   If it snows tomorrow, what will you do?

2. **Ii tenki nara, (anata wa) sampo shimasu ka?**
   If it is good weather, do you take a walk?

3. (Sore ga) Amari takai nara, watakushi wa kaimasen.
   If it is too expensive, I will not buy it.

4. Anata go iku nara, (watakushitachi mo) issho ni ikimashō ka?
   If you go, shall we go together?

5. (Watakushi wa) Sake o nomu to, (watakushi no) kao ga sugu akaku narimasu.
   Whenever I drink sake, my face turns red right away.

6. Tenki ga ii to, (watakushi wa) sampo shimosu.
   Whenever the weather is fine, I take a walk.

NOTES

Another use of the dictionary form of the verb is in combination with a following *nara* to express the English "if" clause or phrase. The word *moshi* might be used before the clause or phrase to add emphasis to the condition.

In Japanese an adjective or a noun is often used to express an idea that in English would also require a verb. In informal, colloquial English we might say, "If cheap, I'll buy it"; but in formal English we would say, "If it is cheap, I will buy it." In Japanese, however, an expression like *Yasui nara kaimasu* is formally adequate. (Again, there are other ways of expressing the "if" idea [Conditional] in Japanese, but we are using here the most simple.)

VOCABULARY

furu (furi-, futte) .... *fall*
(rain or snow)

sampo suru (shi-, shite) ... *take a walk*

ame .... *rain*

yuki .... *snow*

tenki .... *weather*

amari .... *too much*

nedan .... *price*

nara (after the "if" phrase or clause) ... *if (in case that)*

moshi (for emphasis, before the "if" phrase or clause) .... *if*

to (after the "whenever" phrase or clause) .... *whenever*

sugu .... *right away, at once*

EXERCISES

1. Are you going to Hakone next Saturday?

2. Yes, I shall go.

3. How long (until when) will you be there?

4. If the weather is good, I will be there from Saturday afternoon to Monday evening.

5. Where will you be in Hakone?

6. I will probably be in the Hakone Hotel.

7. Isn't that hotel very expensive?

8. If it is too expensive, I will go to my friend's house at Miyanoshita.

9. Whenever I go to Hakone, it always rains.

10. Then let's go to Nikko.

Answers for Lesson 33
appear on page 217

SPEECH PATTERN 40A:

Dōzo hon o kudasai.
Please give me a book.

SPEECH PATTERN 40B:

Dōzo sono hon o yonde kudasai.
Please read that book.

EXAMPLES

1. **Dōzo ringo o kudasai.**
   Please give me some apples.

2. **Dōzo mado o akete kudasai.**
   Please open the window.

3. **Dōzo koko ni kite kudasai.**
   Please come here.

4. **Komban dōzo Nihongo o benkyō shite kudasai.**
   Tonight please study your Japanese.

5. **Dozō shatsu o aratte kudasai.**
   Please wash my shirts.

6. **Dozō kore o shite kudasai.**
   Please do this.

NOTES

In "Useful Expressions" we have learned several expressions containing *kudasai*, expressions that ask some favor for the speaker from the person spoken to. The speaker asks to be given something or asks for something to be done for him. The verb denoting the something to be done is in the *-te* form. The use of *dōzo* just adds that much more politeness to the request, just as in English we would say "Please do me the favor ...."

VOCABULARY

arau (arai-, aratte) ... wash	*kudasai* ...... *please give me*
naosu (naoshi-, naoshite) .... *mend, fix*	*dōzo* .... *please*

EXAMPLES

Express in Japanese:

1. **Please give me the key to my room.**

2. **Is this your key?**

3. No, that is not mine. Mine is in the box on the left.

4. Oh, yes, I have forgotten. Please forgive me.

5. Don't mention it.

6. Will you eat dinner in your room?

7. I think so. If Mr. Smith is here at six o'clock, please bring dinner to my room. How much are these newspapers?

8. Ten yen.

9. Thank you.

10. Will you take a walk this evening?

11. No, I will go to bed early tonight. Please bring breakfast to my room at seven o'clock tomorrow morning.

Answers for Lesson 34
appear on page 218

LESSON 35

SPEECH PATTERN 41A:

(Watakushi wa) Mizu ga hoshii desu.
I want (some) water.

SPEECH PATTERN 41B:

(Watakushi wa) Mizu wa hoshiku arimasen.
I do not want (any) water.

SPEECH PATTERN 42A:

(Watakushi wa) Mizu ga nomitai desu.
I want to drink (some) water.

SPEECH PATTERN 42B:

(Watakushi wa) Mizu wa nomitaku arimasen.
I do not want to drink (any) water.

EXAMPLES

1. **Sakana ga atarashii nara, (watakushi wa) hoshii desu.**
    If the fish are fresh, I want some.

2. **Ashita tenki ga ii nara, (watakushi wa) Nikkō e itikai desu.**
    If the weather is good tomorrow, I want to go to Nikko.

3. **(Anata wa) Nihongo o motto naraitai desu ka?**
    Do you want to learn more Japanese?

4. **Hai, (watakushi wa) yoku naraitai desu.**
    Yes, I want to learn it well.

5. **(Anata wa) Nihongo no jibiki ga hoshii desu ka?**
    Do you want a Japanese dictionary?

6. **Hai, (watakushi wa) ii no ga hoshii desu.**
    Yes, I want a good one.

NOTES

The English expression "I want (something)" or "I do not want (something)" is expressed in Japanese in terms of "(something) is (or is not) desirous." Therefore either the particle *gwa* or *wa*, both of which are related to the subject of the verb, rather than the particle *o*, which is related to the object of the verb, follows the word denoting the something that is wanted.

Notice that the ending *-tai* is added to the "stem" of the verb.

Notice also that the negatives of *hoshii* and the *-tai* ending verb are formed the same way that the negative of "true adjectives" is formed (see Lesson 7), that is, by changing the final *i* to *ku*.

VOCABULARY

dansu .... *dance*	*ojiisan* .... *an old man*
dōmo .... *indeed, very much*	*ryokō* .... *travel*
osoku .... *late (adv.)*	*tempura* ..... *Japanese meat or fish deep fry*
hoshii .... *desirous of having; want (an object)*	*sukiyaki* ..... *Japanese meat and vegetable dish*
-tai .... *verb ending meaning "want to, like to, wish to"*	*no* .... *one (pronoun)*

EXERCISES

Express in Japanese:

1. It has become late. Do you want to eat dinner?

2. Yes, I want to eat dinner.

3. Which do you desire, tempura or sukiyaki?

4. **Please bring me sukiyaki.**

5. **Do you want to dance afterwards?**

6. **No, I do not want to dance tonight. If it is good weather tomorrow, I want to go to Nikko. I want to go to bed early tonight.**

7. **Do you want to go with me in my car?**

8. **Yes, that's excellent. Thank you very much.**

9. **If it is raining, let us go by train.**

**Answers for Lesson 35
appear on page 219**

This lesson is a review designed to determine how well students have learned and how readily they can use the Speech Patterns taught in this book. Responses should be grammatically complete statements. Answers are on pages 225-231.

VOCABULARY

The following words marked by an asterisk have been introduced for the first time in the various pictorial reviews contained in this text.

higashi .... *east*

* *jyoyū* .... *actress*

* *kakaru* .... *take (time)*

* *kirométoru* ...... *kilometer*

* *kita* .... *north*

* *kongetsu* .... *this month*

minami .... *south*

* *mizuumi* .... *lake*

* *nampun* .... *how many minutes?*

nish .... *west*

* *shōbōsho* .... *fire station*

* *suki* .... *like, be fond of*

* *tsumetai* .... *cold*

* *yukkuri* ... *slowly, leisurely*

REVIEW A

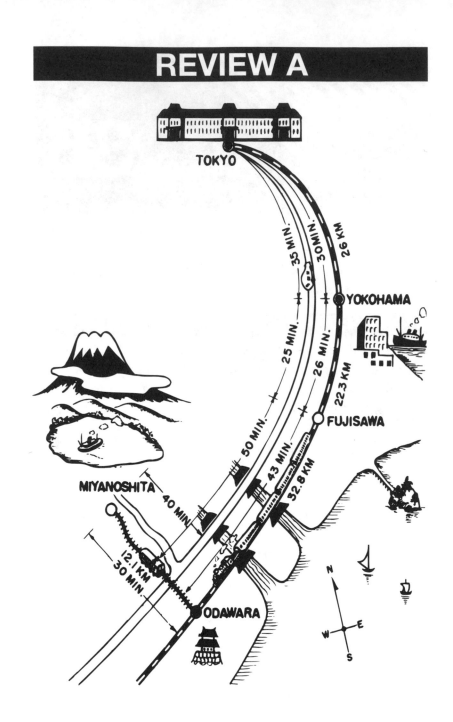

TOKYO

35 MIN. 30 MIN. 26 KM

YOKOHAMA

25 MIN. 26 MIN. 22.3 KM

FUJISAWA

50 MIN. 43 MIN. 32.8 KM

MIYANOSHITA

40 MIN.

12.1 KM
30 MIN.

ODAWARA

N
W E
S

1. Anata wa Tōkyō kara Miyanoshita made kisha de iku koto ga dekimasu ka?

2. Kisha wa odawara kara Tōkyō made ikimasu ka?

3. Jidōsha wa Fujisawa e ikimasu ka?

4. Anata wa Tōkyō kara Miyanoshita made jidōsha de hayaku iku koto ga dekimasu ka? Kisha de hayaku iku koto ga dekimasu ka?

5. Fujisawa wa Yokohama no dochira no hō ni arimasu ka?

6. Odawara wa Tōkyō no kita ni arimasen ka?

7. Mizuumi ni ikutsu fune ga arimasu ka?

8. Dore ga ichiban takai yama desu ka?

9. Anata ga Tōkyō o jidōsha de hiru ni deru to Yokohama e nanji ni tsukimasu ka? Fujisawa e wa? Odawara e wa? Miyanoshita e wa?

10. Anata ga Odawara o gozen kuji ni kisha de deru to nanji ni Tōkyō e tsukimasu ka?

11. Tōkyō kara Yokohama made jidōsha de nampun kakarimasu ka? Yokohama kara Fujisawa made wa? Fujisawa kara Odawara made wa? Odawara kara Miyanoshita made wa?

12. Tōkyō kara Yokohama made nankiromētoru arimasu ka? Yokohama kara Fujusawa made wa? Fujisawa kara Odawara made wa? Odawara kara Miyanoshita made wa?

REVIEW B

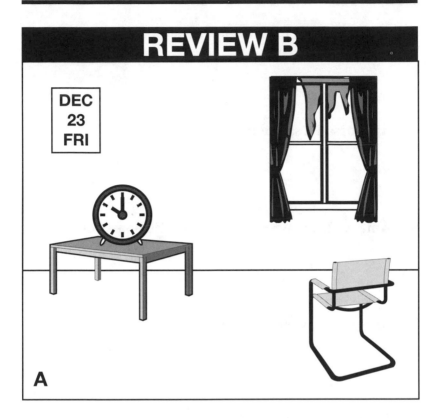

DEC
23
FRI

A

1. Naniyōbi desu ka?

2. Nangatsu desu ka?

3. Nanji desu ka?

4. Tokei wa doko ni arimasu ka?

5. Atsu desu ka samui desu ka?

6. Ame ga futte imasu ka yuki ga futte imasu ka?

7. Asatte wa Easter desu ka?

8. Kesa wa atsui desu ka?

9. Isu wa tēburu no mae ni arimasu ka ushiro ni arimasu ka?

10. Tēburu wa isu yori mo mado no chikaku ni arimasu ka?

1. Sakuban wa yuki ga furimashita ka?

2. Kinō wa nichiyōbi dewa arimasen deshita ka?

3. Ima wa sanji nijuppun sugi desu ka?

4. Hana wa ie no naka ni arimasu ka?

5. Kongetsu wa rokugatsu desu ka shichigatsu desu ka?

6. Heya no naka ni tēburu ga ikutsu arimasu ka?

7. Ashita wa samuku narimashō ka?

8. Ano hito wa tēburu no tokoro e ikimasu ka?

9. Ima wa asa desu ka yūgata desu ka?

10. Anu hito wa shimbun o yomimasu ka?

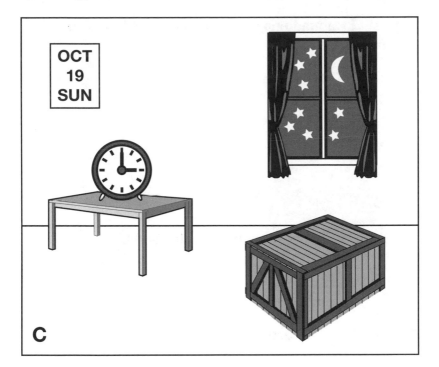

1. Ima wa gozen sanji desu ka gogo sanji desu ka?

2. Watakushi wa ima hataraite imasu ka yasunde imasu ka?

3. Watakushi wa kesa kyōkai e ikimashō ka?

4. Tsuki wa mado no migi ni arimasu ka hidari ni arimasu ka?

5. Kongetsu wa ichigatsu desu ka?

6. Tēburu no ashi wa nambon arimasu ka?

7. Komban wa warui tenki desu ka?

8. Anata wa nanji ni asahan o tabemasu ka? Hiruhan wa? Bangohan wa?

9. Hako wa doko ni arimasu ka?

10. Hako wa ki de tsukurimashita ka?

APR
10
TUE

D

1. Yuki ga futte imsu ka?

2. Sakuban wa suzushiku wa arimasen deshita ka?

3. Kinō wa naniyōbi deshita ka?

4. Watakushi wa kono heya de tabemasu ka?

5. Moshi watakushi ga doyōbi ni hachiji kara jūniji made hataraku nara nanjikan watakushi wa hatarakimasu ka?

6. Anata wa maiasa nanji ni okimasu ka?

7. Kongetsu to gogatsu dewa dochira ga nagai desu ka?

8. Dentō wa doko desu ka? Tēburu wa? Isu wa? Shindai wa?

9. Watakushi wa ima yasunde imasu ka?

10. Heya no naka ni nannin hito ga imasu ka?

REVIEW C

Kono hitotachi wa bīru o nonde imasu. Bīru wa tsumetai desu. Atsui hi desu.

Kono hitotachi wa bīru o nonde imasen. Hiruhan o ryōriya de tabete imasu.

Kono hitotachi wa hataraite imashita. Ima uchi e kaerimasu. Ame ga furu to hatarakimasen. Tenki ga yoi to hatarakimasu.

Kono hito wa hataraite imasen. Ki no shita de yasunde imasu. Goji ni machi e itte bīru o nomimasu.

1. Nannin no hito ga nonde imasu ka?

2. Ano hitotachi wa nani o nonde imasu ka?

3. Otoko no hito wa doko de yasunde imasu ka?

4. Otoko no hito wa goji ni nani o shimasu ka?

5. Tenki ga warui to ano hitotachi wa hatarakimasu ka?

6. Ano hitotachi wa uchi e jitensha de kaerimasu ka?

7. Hayaku aruite imasu ka yukkuri aruite imasu ka?

8. Ryōriya no naka no hitotachi wa nani o shite imasu ka?

9. Migi no hō no hito wa tomodachi e tegami o kaite imasu ka?

10. Anata wa tsumetai bīru ga suki desu ka?

Kono seito wa gakkō e jitensha de kimashita. Hon o motte kimasen deshita.

Kono seito wa ringo o katte sensei ni motte ikimasu. Hon o migi no te ni motte imasu.

Kono seitotachi wa aruite kimashita. Eigo o benkyō shimasu.

Kono otoko no ko wa imōto o gakkō e issho ni tsurete ikimasu. Imoto wa gakkō e ikitaku arimasen.

1. Seito wa nannin gakkō e aruite ikimashita ka?

2. Dochira no seito ga gakkō e jidōsha de kimashita ka?

3. Onna no ko wa otoko no ko yori chiisai desu ka ōkii
desu ka?

4. Otoko no ko wa dochira no te ni ringo o motte imasu
ka?

5. Hon o dochira no te ni motte imasu ka?

6. Seito no bōshi wa doko ni arimasu ka?

7. Kono gakkō de seito wa nani o benkyō shimasu ka?

8. Anata wa kono heya de nani o benkyō shimasu ka?

9. Anata wa Nihongo o yomu koto to kaku koto ga
dekimasu ka?

10. Maiban benkyō shitai desu ka?

Tokyo tower

Peace memorial park

APPENDIX A

Summary of Modifying Words

TYPE A

Modifying words (true adjectives) are not followed by any particle in affirmative sentences (Examples 1 & 2). Modifying words are not followed by any particle in negative sentences when they precede a noun they modify (Example 3). They are used as the same type of words in English. In negative sentences, however, when they do not precede a noun, they may be followed by *wa* (Example 4). In this case, the final *i* of the modifying word is changed to *ku*.

EXAMPLES

1. **Kore-wa ōkii hako des´.**
   This is a big box.

2. **Kono hako-wa ōkii des´.**
   This box is big.

3. **Kore-wa ōkii hako dewa arimasen.**
   This is not a big box.

4. **Kono hako-wa ōkiku(wa) arimasen.**
   This box is not big.

Adjective Form	Meaning	Negative
akai	red	akaku
aoi	blue	aoku
atarashii	new; fresh	atarashiku
atatakai	warm	atatakaku
atsui	hot	atsuku
chiisai	little; small	chiisaku
furui	old	furuku
hiroi	broad; wide	hiroku
ii (yoi)	good	yoku
karui	light	karuku
kiiroi	yellow	kiiroku
kuroi	black	kuroku
mijikai	short	mijikaku
nagai	long	nagaku
ōkii	large; big	ōkiku
omoi	heavy	omoku
omoshiroi	interesting	omoshiroku
samui	cold	samuku
semai	narrow	semaku
shiroi	white	shiroku
suzashii	cool	suzushiku
takai	expensive; high	takaku
utsukushii	beautiful	utsukushiku
warui	bad	waruku
yasashii	easy	yasashiku
yasui	cheap	yasuku
yowai	weak	yowaku
yoi	good	yoku

TYPE B

These modifying words (quasi-adjectives) are followed by *na* when they precede a noun they modify (Example 1 & 3). In negative sentences, they do not change in form; however, they are followed by *dewa arimasen* (Example 3 & 4).

EXAMPLES

1. **Kore-wa kirei-na heya des´.**
   This is a clean room.

2. **Kono heya-wa kirei des´.**
   This room is clean.

3. **Kore-wa kirei-na heya dewa arimasen.**
   This isn't a clean room.

4. **Kono heya-wa kirei dewa arimasen.**
   This room is not clean.

   jōbu (na) .... *healthy; strong; sturdy; solid*
   jōzu (na) .... *skillful; good at*
   kirei (na) .... *pretty; fine looking; clean*
   rikō (na) .... *intelligent; clever; wise*

APPENDIX B

Regular, Semi-Regular & Irregular Verbs

The following tables contain all the verbs taken up in this book, plus a few more.

For our purpose we divide the Japanese verb into three groups:

A. **Regular**
B. **Semi-regular**
C. **Irregular**

Group A is further divided into six sub-groups. Note that these six sub-groups of Group A contain verbs with the following final syllables:

Group 1. *-gu and -ku*
Group 2. *-su*
Group 3. *-tsu*
Group 4. *-bu, -mu, -nu*
Group 5. *-ru*
Group 6. *-u*

These sub-groups determine the manner of forming the *-te* form of the verbs of **Group A** (Regular).

Note that the dictionary forms of the **Group B** verbs end with *-eru* or *-iru*. All but a few Japanese verbs that end with *-eru* and *-iru* belong to this group.

The two verbs listed in **Group C** (*kuru* and *suru*) are the only irregular verbs in Japanese.

Group A: Regular verbs

Dictionary Form	*Base*	*-te Form*
1. *-ku, -gu*		
iku (go)	*iki-*	*itte*
isogu (hurry)	*isogi-*	*isoide*
aruku (walk)	*aruki-*	*aruite*
hataraku (work)	*hataraki-*	*hataraite*
kaku (write or draw)	*kaki-*	*kaite*
kiku (hear)	*kiki-*	*kiite*
tsuku (arrive)	*tsuki-*	*tsuite*
ugoku (move)	*ugoki-*	*ugoite*
yuku (go)	*yuki-*	*itte*
2. *-su*		
hanasu (speak, talk, tell)	*hanashi-*	*hanashite*
kasu (lend)	*kashi-*	*kashite*
naosu (fix, mend)	*naoshi-*	*naoshite*

Dictionary Form	*Base*	*-te Form*

3. *-tsu*

motsu (hold, have)	mochi-	motte
tatsu (stand up)	tachi-	tatte

4. *-bu, -mu, -nu*

yobu (call)	yobi-	yonde
yomu (read)	yomi-	yonde
nomu (drink)	nomi-	nonde
yasumu (rest, go to bed)	yasumi-	yasunde
shinu (die)	shini-	shinde

5. *-ru*

aru (am, is, are)	ari-	atte
furu (fall [rain, snow])	furi-	futte
iru (to be, exist)	i-	ite
iru (need)	iri-	itte
kakaru (take, cost)	kakari-	kakatte
naru (become)	nari-	natte
nemuru (sleep)	nemuri-	nemutte
okuru (send)	okuri-	okutte
toru (take)	tori-	totte
tsukuru (make)	tsukuri-	tsukutte
uru (sell)	uri-	utte
wakaru (understand)	wakari-	wakatte

Dictionary Form	*Base*	*-te Form*
6. -u		
arau (wash)	*arai-*	*aratte*
iu (say, speak)	*ii-*	*itte*
kau (buy)	*kai-*	*katte*
narau (learn)	*narai-*	*naratte*

Group B: Semi-Regular verbs

Dictionary Form	*Base*	*-te Form*
-eru		
akeru (open)	*ake-*	*akete*
ageru (give)	*age-*	*agete*
dekakeru (go out)	*dekake-*	*dekakete*
deru (go out, come out)	*de-*	*dete*
machigaeru (make a mistake)	*machigae-*	*machigaete*
oshieru (teach)	*oshie-*	*oshiete*
shimeru (close)	*shime-*	*shimete*
taberu (eat)	*tabe-*	*tabete*
tateru (build)	*tate-*	*tatete*
wasureru (forget)	*wasure-*	*wasurete*
-iru		
dekiru (can do)	*deki-*	*dekite*
miru (see)	*mi-*	*mite*
okiru (get up from bed)	*oki-*	*okite*

Group C: Irregular verbs

Dictionary Form	Base	-te Form
kuru (come)	ki-	kite
suru (do)	shi	shite

SUMMARY OF VERB FORMS

The following four verb endings have been introduced in this book:

- masu .... *Affirmative form for simple present and definite future.*

- masen .... *Negative form for simple present or definite future.*

- mashita .... *Affirmative form for simple past.*

- masen deshita .... *Negative form for simple past.*

Dictionary Form and Meaning	Base	Simple Present & Definite Future		
		Affirmative	**Negative**	
iru (to be)	*i*	*imasu*	*imasen*	
aru (to be)	*ari*	*arimasu (desu)*	*de arimasen*	
oru (to be)	*ori*	*(or) imasu*	*(or) imasen*	
akeru (to open)	*ake*	*akemasu*	*akemasen*	
hanasu (to speak)	*hanashi*	*hanashimasu*	*hanashimasen*	
iku (to go)	*iki*	*ikimasu*	*ikimasen*	
iru (to need)	*iri*	*irimasu*	*irimasen*	
isogu (to hurry)	*isogi*	*isogimasu*	*isogimasen*	
kaku (to write)	*kaki*	*kakimasu*	*kakimasen*	
kau (to buy)	*kai*	*kaimasu*	*kaimasen*	
kuru (to come)	*ki*	*kimasu*	*kimasen*	
machigau (to make a mistake)	*machigae*	*machigaemasu*	*machigaemasen*	
miru (to see)	*mi*	*mimasu*	*mimasen*	
nomu (to drink)	*nomi*	*nomimasu*	*nomimasen*	
shimeru (to close)	*shime*	*shimemasu*	*shimemasen*	
taberu (to eat)	*tabe*	*tabemasu*	*tabemasen*	
tsuku (to arrive)	*tsuki*	*tsukimasu*	*tsukimasen*	
wakaru (to understand)	*wakari*	*wakarimasu*	*wakarimasen*	
wasureru (to forget)	*wasure*	*wasuremasu*	*wasuremasen*	
yomu (to read)	*yomi*	*yomimasu*	*yomimasen*	

Dictionary Form and Meaning	Base	Simple Past Affirmative	Negative
iru (to be)	i	imashita	imasen deshita
aru (to be)	ari	arimashita (deshita)	arimasen deshita
oru (to be)	ori	(or) imashita	(or) imasen deshita
akeru (to open)	ake	akemashita	akemasen deshita
hanasu (to speak)	hanashi	hanashimashita	hanashimasen deshita
iku (to go)	iki	ikimashita	ikimasen deshita
iru (to need)	iri	irimashita	irimasen deshita
isogu (to hurry)	isogi	isogimashita	isogimasen deshita
kaku (to write)	kaki	kakimashita	kakimasen deshita
kau (to buy)	kai	kaimashita	kaimasen deshita
kuru (to come)	ki	kimashita	kimasen deshita
machigau (to make a mistake)	machigae	machigaemashita	machigaemasen deshita
miru (to see)	mi	mimashita	mimasen deshita
nomu (to drink)	nomi	nomimashita	nomimasen deshita
shimeru (to close)	shime	shimemashita	shimemasen deshita
taberu (to eat)	tabe	tabemashita	tabemasen deshita
tsuku (to arrive)	tsuki	tsukimashita	tsukimasen deshita
wakaru (to understand)	wakari	wakarimashita	wakarimasen deshita
wasureru (to forget)	wasure	wasuremashita	wasuremasen deshita
yomu (to read)	yomi	yomimashita	yomimasen deshita

APPENDIX C

Summary of Particles

In Japanese there is an important group of words called in this course "particles." Their purpose is to show the relation of one word to another, or to connect the different parts of a sentence. Many particles correspond to several different English words, depending on the way they are used in particular sentences. Some particles cannot be translated into English at all. The best way to learn the use and meaning of particles is to learn them in phrases and sentences, and to remember the meaning of the whole expression.

1. **ga (11)** .... *Places emphasis on subject.*

2. **ka (2, 8)** .... *Indicates a question.*

3. **na (6)** .... *Used with certain abstract nouns which modify other nouns.*

4. **no (4, 5, & 6)** .... *Used with certain nouns which modify other nouns; indicates possession.*

5. **o (16)** .... *Used after direct object.*

6. **wa (1, 7)** .... *Indicates the subject of the sentence; singles out certain locations and time from other possible locations and time.*

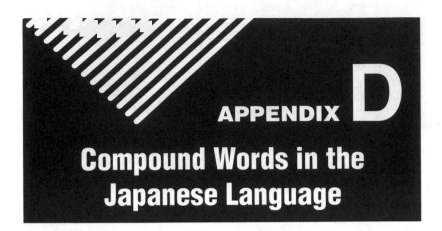

APPENDIX D

Compound Words in the Japanese Language

Many Japanese words are combinations of two independent words joined together in one word. Sometimes the first letters of the second part are changed to effect greater ease in pronunciation. The following is a list of compound words which appear in the vocabulary of this part, together with the component parts.

asagohan .... breakfast	*asa* .... morning	*gohan* .... meal
ashikubi .... ankle	*ashi* .... foot	*kubi* .... neck
bangohan .... dinner	*ban* .... evening	*gohan* .... meal
deguchi .... exit	*deru* .... leave	*kuchi* .... mouth
densha .... streetcar	*den* .... electric	*sha* .... wheel
empitsu .... pencil	*en* .... lead	*hitsu* .... brush
haizara .... ashtray	*hai* .... ash	*sara* .... dish
hibachi ..... fire brazier	*hi* .... fire	*hachi* .... low vase
hirugohan .... lunch	*hiru* .... noon	*gohan* .... meal
hombako ..... bookcase	*hon* .... book	*hako* .... box
honya .... bookstore	*hon* .... book	*ya* .... store
iriguchi .... entrance	*iru* .... come	*kuchi* .... mouth
kakemono ..... hanging scroll	*kakeru* .... hang	*mono* .... thing

kamisori .... *razor*	*kami* .... *hair*	*soru* .... *shave*
kusuriya ...... *drugstore*	*kusuri* .... *medicine*	*ya* .... *store*
mannenhitsu ... *fountain*	*mannen* .. *ten thousand*	*hitsu* .... *brush*
pen	*year*	
megane ..... *spectacles*	*me* .... *eye*	*kagami* .... *mirror*
nagagutsu .... *long boots*	*nagai* .... *long*	*kutsu* .... *shoes*
nurimono . *lacquerware*	*nuru* .... *paint*	*mono* .... *thing*
okimono ...... *ornament*	*oku* .... *put*	*mono* .... *thing*
ryōriya ...... *restaurant*	*ryōri* .... *cookery*	*ya* .... *store*
shitamachi ... *downtown*	*shita* .... *down*	*machi* .... *town*
suimono .... *soup*	*suu* .... *sip*	*mono* .... *thing*
tabemono .... *food*	*taberu* .... *eat*	*mono* .... *thing*
tatemono .... *building*	*tateru* .... *build*	*mono* .... *thing*
tegami .... *letter*	*te* .... *hand*	*kami* .... *paper*
tekubi .... *wrist*	*te* .... *hand*	*kubi* .... *neck*
todana .... *closet*	*to* .... *door*	*tana* .... *shelf*
tokidoki ..... *sometimes*	*toki* .... *time*	*toki* .... *time*
yubiwa .... *ring*	*yubi* .... *finger*	*wa* .... *circle*

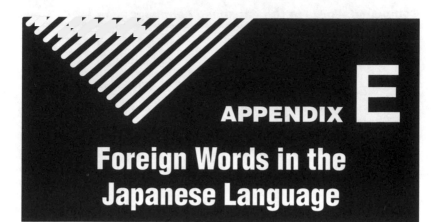

The following is a list of some foreign words which the Japanese have adopted into their language with little change in pronunciation. It is safe to assume that all the words in this list are understood and used by the Japanese who have no knowledge of English as a language. This list can be expanded as the student gains experience in conversing with Japanese.

alcohol .... *arakoru*

all right .... *orai*

apartment .... *apato*

apron .... *epuron*

ball .... *boru*

banana .... *banana*

bar (drinking place) ...... *ba*

baseball .... *besuboru*

basket .... *basuketto*

basketball ... *basuketto boru*

bat (baseball) .... *batto*

bed .... *betto*

beefsteak .... *bifuteki*

beer .... *biiru*

belt .... *beruto*

bench .... *benchi*

boat .... *boto*

bonus .... *bonasu*

building .... *biru*

bus .... *basu*

button .... *botan*

cafe .... *kafue*

cake .... *keiki*

calendar .... *kalenda*

camp	kyampu	**gasoline**	gasorin
can (container)	kan	**glass (substance)**	garasu
card	kado	**group**	gurupu
catalogue	katarogu	**guitar**	gita
cement	semento	**hall (auditorium)**	horu
cheese	chizu	**ham**	hamu
chewing gum	chuin gamu	**handkerchief**	hankachi
chocolate	chokoreto	**handle**	handoru
circus	sakasu	**hiking**	haikingu
club	kurabu	**hook**	hokku
cocoa	kokoa	**hotel (western style)**	hoteru
coffee	kohi	**ice**	aisu
cook	kokku	**ice cream**	aisukurimu
cream	kurimu	**inch**	inchi
cup	koppu	**ink**	inku
dance	dansu	**iron (flat iron)**	airon
department store	depato	**jam (food)**	jamu
door	doa	**jazz**	jazu
elevator	erebeta	**knife**	naifu
engine	enjin	**lamp**	rampu
feet	fito	**lemon**	remon
film	firumu	**lion**	raion
football	futto boru	**manager**	maneja
fork	hoku	**match**	mat´chi
fry	furai	**milk**	miruku
game	gemu	**model**	moderu

modern	*modan (na)*	*poster*	*posuta*
motor boat	*mota boto*	*program*	*puroguramu*
napkin	*nafukin*	*pump*	*pompu*
news	*nyusu*	*radio*	*rajio*
notebook	*notobukku*	*raincoat*	*renkoto*
O.K.	*O´kei*	*record (phonograph)*	*rekodo*
opera	*opera*	*ribbon*	*ribon*
orange	*orenji*	*rocket*	*roketto*
orchestra	*okesutora*	*rucksack*	*rikkusakku*
organ (music)	*orugan*	*sandwich*	*sandoit´chi*
overcoat	*oba*	*sauce*	*sosu*
page	*peji*	*sausage*	*soseji*
paint	*penki*	*searchlight*	*sachiraito*
pajama	*pajama*	*shovel*	*shaberu*
pamphlet	*panfuretto*	*skate*	*suketo*
pants (under)	*pantsu*	*sketch book*	*suket´chi bukku*
parachute	*parashuto*	*ski*	*sukii*
pen	*pen*	*skirt*	*sukato*
piano	*piyano*	*soda*	*soda*
picnic	*pikunikku*	*soup*	*supu*
pin	*pm*	*sports*	*supotsu*
pineapple	*painappuru*	*spy*	*supai*
ping pong	*pin pon*	*stamp*	*sutampu*
pipe	*paipu*	*stop*	*sutoppu*
pistol	*pisutoru*	*stove*	*sutobu*
pool (swimming)	*puru*	*strike*	*sutoraiku*

tank	*tanku*	*tulip*	*churippu*
taxi	*takushii*	*tunnel*	*tonneru*
television	*terebijon*	*typewriter*	*taipuraita*
tennis	*tenisu*	*typhoon*	*taifu*
tent	*tento*	*violin*	*baiorin*
tire	*taiya*	*vitamin*	*bitamin*
toast	*tosuto*	*whisky*	*uisuki*
tomato	*tomato*	*yacht*	*yotto*
towel	*taoru*	*zero*	*zero*
truck	*torakku*		

Answers for Lesson 18
Speech Pattern Review

This section contains Japanese answers for the Exercises for the *Speech Pattern Review* in Lesson 18.

REVIEW A

PICTURE 1

a.   *Iie, ano ko wa Amerika no otoko no ko dewa arimasen. Ano ko wa Nihon no otoko no ko desu.*

b.   *Iie, ano otoko no ko wa Amerikajin dewa arimasen. Ano ko wa Nihonjin desu.*

PICTURE 2

a.   *Hai, sore wa hen na tori desu.*

b.   *Hai, kono tori wa hen desu.*

PICTURE 3

a. *Iie, anata no okane wa kin dewa arimasen. Sore wa kami desu.*

b. *Iie, anata no wa kin no okane dewa arimasen. Sore wa kami no okane desu.*

PICTURE 4

a. *Iie, ano kirei no onna no hito wa gakkō no sensei dewa arimasen. Ano hito wa jyoyū desu.*

b. *Hai, ano onna no hito wa kirei desu.*

PICTURE 5

a. *Hai, kono otoko no hito wa jōbu desu.*

b. *Hai, kono hito wa jōbu na otoko no hito desu.*

PICTURE 6

Iie, kesa no tenki wa yoku arimasen. Warui desu.

PICTURE 7

a.   *Hai, sore wa kiiroi dentō dewa arimasen. Akai dentō desu.*

b.   *Iie, kono dentō wa kiiro dewa arimasen. Akai desu.*

PICTURE 8

Iie, sore wa machi no keisatsusho dewa arimasen. Machi no shōbōsho desu.

PICTURE 9

a.   *Hai, kyō wa atatakai hi dewa arimasen. Samui hi desu.*

b.   *Iie, kyō wa atatakaku arimasen. Samui desu.*

REVIEW B

1. *Kono e no naka ni tsukue ga hitotsu arimasu.*

2. *Isu wa tsukue no mae ni arimasu.*

3. *Tsukue no shita ni neko ga imasu.*

4. *Yuka wa isu no shita ni arimasu.*

5. *Iie, mado wa tsukue no ushiro ni arimasu.*

6. *Tsukue no ue ni tegami to sara ga arimasu.*

7. *Sumisu san ga tegami o kakimashita.*

8. *Jōnzu san wa Tōkyō ni imasu.*

9. *Sara no naka ni ringo ga futatsu arimasu.*

10. *Dentō wa tsukue no ue ni arimasu.*

11. *Tsukue wa isu to kabe no aida ni arimasu.*

12. *Iie, sumisu san wa kono heya ni imasen.*

13. *Iie, tsukue no ue ni denwa wa arimasen.*

14. *Iie, tegami to sara wa yuka no ue ni arimasen. Tsukue no ue ni arimasu.*

15. *Hai, mado wa tsukue no soba ni arimasu.*

Answers for Exercises, Lessons 19-26, 28-35

This section contains Japanese translations for the Exercises for Lessons 19 through 35.

LESSON 19 EXERCISES

1. I wrote a letter this morning.
   Watakushi wa keso tegami o kakimashita.

2. To whom did you send it?
   Dare ni sore o okurimashita ka?

3. I sent it to my father.
   Chichi ni okurimashita.

4. Where is your father?
   (Anato no) Otōsan wa doko ni imasu ka?

5. He is in Osaka. He is coming to Tokyo tomorrow.
   Ōsaka ni imasu. Ashita Tōkyō e kimasu.

6. My father sold that house (over there) to Mr. Tanaka.
   Chichi wa Tanaka san ni ano ie o urimashita.

7. Is your mother in Osaka?
    Okāsan wa Ōsaka ni imasu ka?

8. No, my mother is not in Osaka.
    Iie, haha wa Ōsaka ni imasen.

9. She came to Tokyo yesterday.
    Kinō Tōkyō e kimashita.

10. My mother teaches English to my wife.
    Haha wa Eigo o kanai ni oshiemasu.

LESSON 20 EXERCISES

1. How many apples are there on the table?
    Tēburu no ue ni ringo ga ikutsu arimasu ka?

2. There are nine apples.
    Ringo ga kokonotsu arimasu.

3. Did you give an apple to that child?
    Sono kodomo ni ringo o hitotsu agemashita ka?

4. I did not give an apple.
    Watakushi wa ringo o agemasen deshita.

5. I am going to give five cakes now.
    Ima okashi o itsutsu agemasu.

6. How many pencils are there in the box now?
    Ima hako no naka ni ikutsu empitsu ga arimasu ka?

7. There are ten. There are five on the desk.
    Tō arimasu. Tsukue no ue ni itsutsu arimasu.

8. Tomorrow I shall give four pencils and six notebooks
    to my Japanese friend.
    *Ashita watakushi wa Nihonjin no tomodachi ni
    empitsu o yottsu to chōmen o muttsu agemasu.*

9. That is good. Now I will give you three of these apples.
    *Sore wa yoi desu. Ima watakushi ga anata ni ringo o
    mittsu agemasu.*

10. Thank you very much. Will you come to my house today?
    *Dōmo arigatō gozaimasu. Kyō anata wa watakushi no
    uchi e kimasu ka?*

11. I am sorry. Today I go to school.
    Gomen nasai. Kyō watakushi wa gakko e yukimasu.

12. Oh, I see. I have forgotten. Will you come to my
    house tomorrow?
    *Aa sō desu ka? Watakushi wa wasuremashita. Ashita
    anata wa watakushi no uchi e kimasu ka?*

13. Yes. Thank you very much.
    Hai. Arigatō gozaimasu.

LESSON 21 EXERCISES

1. When is Mr. Brown coming to Tokyo?
    Buraun san wa itsu Tōkyō e kimasu ka?

2. He will (probably) come the day after tomorrow.
    (Ano hito wa) Asotte kimashō.

3. Mr. Smith will probably come tonight.
   Sumisu san wa tabun komban kimashō.

4. Let us take (eat) a meal together with him tomorrow.
   Ashita ano hito to issho ni gohan o tabemashō.

5. Mr. Tanaka and Mr. Brown will probably come together.
   Tanaka san to Buraun san wa tabun issho ni kimashō.

6. Is that so?
   Sō desu ka?

7. Yes, they will probably arrive in the morning.
   Hai, ano hitotachi wa tabun asa tsukimashō.

8. Then probably the next day Mr. Tanaka, together with Mr. Brown, will go to Tokyo.
   Sorekara tabun yokujitsu Tanaka san wa Buraun san to issho ni Tōkyō e ikimashō.

9. I think so. When shall we eat?
   Sō omoimasu. Itsu watakushitachi wa tabemashō ka?

10. Let us eat early in the evening.
    Yugata tabemashō.

LESSON 22 EXERCISES

1. I went to Kamakura yesterday.
   Kinō Kamakura e ikimashita.

2. Did you go by electric train?
   Densha de ikimashita ka?

3. No, I went by car.
Iie, jidōsha de ikimashita.

4. What did you see at Kamakura?
Nani o Kamakura de mimashita ka?

5. I saw the Great Buddha.
Daibutsu o mimashita.

6. Where did you eat dinner?
Doko de bangohan o tabemashita ka?

7. I ate dinner at home.
Uchi de bangohan o tabemashita.

8. Then I heard music on the radio.
Sorekara rajio de ongaku o kikimashita.

9. Afterwards I wrote a letter to my mother with my new fountain pen.
Sorekora watakushi wa watakushi no atarashii mannenhitsu de haha ni tegami o kakimashita.

10. Then I went to a movie with my friend.
Sorekara watakushi wa watakushi no tomodachi to eiga e ikimashita.

LESSON 23 EXERCISES

1. How many houses are there in this town?
Kono machi ni ie wa ikutsu arimasu ka?

2. There are three hundred forty-two houses.
   Uchi ga sambyaku yonjū-ni arimasu.

3. How many people are there?
   Hito wa nannin imasu ka?

4. There are one thousand five hundred people in this town.
   Kono machi ni wa hito ga sen gohyakunin imasu.

5. How many sheets of paper are in the box?
   Hako no naka ni kami ga nanmai arimasu ka?

6. Six sheets.
   Rokumai arimasu.

7. Are there pencils in the box?
   Hako no naka ni empitsu ga arimasu ka?

8. Yes, there are five pencils in the box.
   Hai, hako no naka ni empitsu ga gohon arimasu.

9. How many red pencils are in the box?
   Hako no naka ni akai empitsu wa nambon arimasu ka?

10. Three.
    Sambon arimasu.

11. There are no yellow pencils in the box, are there?
    Hako no naka ni kiiroi empitsu wa arimasen ka?

12. No, there are none.
    Hai, arimasen.

LESSON 24 EXERCISES

1. What time did you leave Tokyo station yesterday?
   Kinō Tōkyō eki o nanji ni demashita ka?

2. I left at 10:15 A.M.
   Gozen jūji jūgofun ni demashita.

3. When did you arrive here?
   Koko ni itsu tsukimashita ka?

4. I arrived here at 3:20 P.M.
   Gogo sanji nijippun ni tsukimashita.

5. Until when will you be here?
   Itsu made koko ni imasu ka?

6. I shall (probably) be here until tomorrow.
   Koko ni ashita made imashō.

7. Will you depart tomorrow morning or tomorrow afternoon?
   Anata wa ashita no asa dekakemasu ka gogo dekakemasu ka?

8. I shall be here until noon tomorrow.
   (Watakushi) wa ashita no hiru made koko ni imasu.

9. Will you go by electric train?
   Anata wa densha de ikimasu ka?

10. Yes, on the 1:30 train.
    Hai, ichiji han no densha de ikimasu.

LESSON 25 EXERCISES

1. What time will you go out tonight?
   Anata wa komban nanji ni dekakemasu ka?

2. I will go out at six o'clock.
   Watakushi wa rokuji ni dekakemasu.

3. Shall we go to Kamakura next Sunday?
   Tsugi no Nichiyōbi ni Kamakura e ikimashō ka?

4. Let's go there next Saturday afternoon.
   Tsugi no Doyōbi no gogo asoko e ikimashō.

5. Don't you work on Saturday?
   Anata wa Doyōbi ni hatarakimasen ka?

6. I don't work every Saturday.
   Watakushi wa maidoyōbi hatarakimasen.

7. How many hours do you work from Monday to Friday?
   Anata wa Getsuyōbi kara Kinyōbi made nanjikan hatarakimasu ka?

8. Forty hours.
   Yonjūjikan desu.

9. Don't you work every day of the week?
   Anata wa isshukan mainichi hatarakimasen ka?

10. No, I rest on Sunday.
    Hai, watakushi wa Nichiyōbi ni yasumimasu.

LESSON 26 EXERCISES

1. When did you go to Kyoto?
   Itsu anata wa Kyōto e ikimashita ka?

2. I went in June.
   Watakushi wa Rokugatsu ni ikimashita.

3. Was it hot in Kyoto? (Was Kyoto hot?)
   Kyōto wa otsui deshita ka?

4. It was not very hot. August will (probably) be hotter.
   Taihen atsuku (wa) arimasen deshita. Hachigatsu wa motto atsui deshō.

5. Was Kyoto hotter than Tokyo?
   Kyōto wa Tōkyō yori atsui deshita ka?

6. Yes, it was (hotter).
   Hai, atsui deshita.

7. Did you go to Nara, too?
   Anata wa Nara e mo ikimashita ka?

8. Yes, I went there too.
   Hai, watakushi wa asoko e mo ikimashita.

9. Which is more beautiful, Tokyo or Kyoto?
   Tōkyō to Kyōto to dochira ga utsukushii desu ka?

10. Kyoto is more beautiful. Kyoto is the most beautiful town in Japan.
    Kyōto no hō ga utsukushii desu. Kyōto wa Nippon no naka de ichiban utukushii machi desu.

11. Which is the largest town, Tokyo, Kyoto or Nara?
    Tōkyō to Kyōto to Nara no naka de dore ga ichiban okii machi desu ka?

12. Tokyo is the largest.
    Tōkyō ga ichiban ōkii desu.

LESSON 28 EXERCISES

1. Can you go to Tokyo tomorrow?
   Ashita Tōkyō e iku koto ga dekumasu ka?

2. No. I cannot go tomorrow.
   Iie, ashita iku koto ga dekimasen.

3. Shall we go on Wednesday?
   Suiyōbi ni ikimashō ka?

4. I cannot go on Wednesday. I will read this book on that day.
   Suiyōbi ni iku koto ga dekimasen. Watakushi wa sono hi ni kono hon o yomimasu.

5. Can you read a Japanese book?
   Nihongo no hon o yomu koto ga dekimasu ka?

6. No, I cannot read Japanese.
   Iie, watakushi wa Nihongo o yomu koto ga dekimasen.

7. Can you speak Japanese?
   Anata wa Nihongo o hanasu koto ga dekimasu ka?

8. I can speak Japanese a little. I can also understand a little.
    Watakushi wa Nihongo o sukoshi hanasu koto ga
    dekimasu. Watakushi wa sukoshi wakaru koto mo
    dekimasu.

9. Can't you write Japanese?
    Anata wa Nihongo o kaku koto ga dekimasen ka?

10. No, I cannot read nor write Japanese.
    Hai, watakushi wa Nihongo o yomu koto mo kaku koto
    mo dekimasen.

LESSON 29 EXERCISES

1. I am going to the bookstore early tomorrow morning.
    Watakushi wa ashita no asa hayaku honya e ikimasu.

2. Is that so? At what time?
    Sō desu ka? Nanji ni?

3. At eight o'clock. I can buy books cheaply there tomorrow.
    Hachiji ni (desu). Ashita watakushi wa soko de hon o
    yasuku kau koto ga dekimasu.

4. Do you read Japanese easily?
    Anata wa Nihongo o yasashiku yomu koto ga
    dekimasu ka?

5. Yes, I can read it well. I cannot write skillfully.
    Hai, watakushi wa sore o yoku yomu koto ga
    dekimasu. Jōzu ni kaku koto ga dekimasen.

6. Is the bookstore far?
    Honya wa tōi desu ka?

7. Yes, it is far. But I can go there quickly in my car.
   Hai, tōi desu. Watakushi no jidōsha de hayaku iku koto ga dekimasu.

8. Shall we go together?
   Issho ni ikimoshō ka?

9. Yes. Let's do that.
   Hai, sō shimashō.

10. Then let's go to bed soon.
    So ekara sugu yasumimashō.

LESSON 30 EXERCISES

1. Will the weather become good tomorrow?
   Tenki ga ashita yoku narimasu ka?

2. I don't think so. The weather is not good in June.
   Watakushi wa sō omoimasen. Rokugatsu no otenki wa yoku arimasen.

3. Is the weather in Japan not good?
   Nihon no tenki wa yoku arimasen ka?

4. In the spring there are warm days and cool days. In March, April, and May there is not much rain. But in June, the weather becomes bad. From June to July there is much rain. In July, the weather becomes very hot.
   Haru ni wa atatakai hi to suzushii hi ga arimasu. Sangatsu to Shigatsu to Gogatsu ni amari ame wa arimasen. Rokugatsu ni wa warui tenki ni narimasu. Rokugatsu kara Shichigatsu made takusan ame ga furimasu. Shichigatsu ni taihen atsuku narimasu.

5. Doesn't Tokyo become very hot in summer?
   Tōkyō wa natsu ni taihen atsuku narimasen ka?

6. Yes, it becomes very hot. In July and August many
   people go to the seaside and to the mountains.
   *Iie, taihen atsuku narimasu. Shichigatsu to
   Hachigatsu ni takusan no hitobito ga kaigan to
   yama e ikimasu.*

7. When does it become cool?
   Itsu suzushiku narimasu ka?

8. In September the weather again becomes cool.
   Kugatsu ni tenki wa mata suzushiku narimasu.

9. Isn't autumn in Japan very beautiful?
   Nihon no aki wa utsukushiku arimasen ka?

10. Yes, Japan becomes beautiful in the autumn. The trees in
    the mountains turn red.
    *Iie, Nihon wa aki ni utsukushiku narimasu. Yama no ki
    wa akaku narimasu.*

11. Does it get cold in winter?
    Fuyu ni samuku narimasu ka?

12. Yes, I think so. It becomes very cold in December,
    January, and February. It also snows very much.
    *Hai, sō omoimasu. Jūnigatsu to Ichigatsu to Nigatsu
    wa taihen samuku narimasu. Yuki mo takusan
    furimasu.*

LESSON 31 EXERCISES

1. What are you doing?
   Nani o shite imasu ka?

2. I am writing a letter to my father.
   Chichi ni tegami o kaite imasu.

3. Where is your father?
   Otōsan wa doko ni imasu ka?

4. He is working in Tokyo.
   Tōkyō de hataraite imasu.

5. How long (from when) has he been working in Tokyo?
   Itsu kara Tōkyō de hataraite imasu ka?

6. He was working in Yokohama until September. Then he went to Tokyo.
   Kugatsu made Yokohama de hataraite imashita.
   Sorekara Tōkyō e ikimashita.

7. Can you go to Tokyo with me the day after tomorrow?
   Asatte anata wa watakushi to issho ni Tōkyō e iku koto ga dekimasu ka?

8. No, I cannot go. I am teaching every day in a Japanese school.
   Iie, watakushi wa iku koto ga dekimasen. Watakushi wa mainichi Nihon no gakkō de oshiete imasu.

9. Oh, I see. Are you going to Tokyo soon?
   Aa sō desu ka? Anata wa sugu Tōkyō ikimasu ka?

10. No, I will be in Kyoto until autumn.
    Iie, watakushi wa Kyōto ni aki made imasu.

11. Then where are you going?
    Sorekara anata wa doko e ikimasu ka?

12. I am probably going to school in America.
    Watakushi wa tabun Amerika no gakkō e ikimashō.

LESSON 32 EXERCISES

1. Are you going to take your camera to Kamakura?
   Anata wa anata no shashinki o Kamakura e motte ikimasu ka?

2. No, I am not taking mine. Can you bring yours?
   Iie, watakushi wa watakushi no wa motte ikimasen. Anata wa anata no o motte kuru koto ga dekimasu ka?

3. Yes, I will bring mine. Are you going to take your lunch?
   Hai, watakushi wa watakushi no o motte ikimasu. Anata wa hirugohan (obentō) o motte ikimasu ka?

4. No, I will buy lunch at a restaurant in Kamakura.
   Iie, watakushi wa hirugohan o Kamakura no ryōriya de kaimasu.

5. Are you going by car or on foot?
   Anata wa jidōsha de ikimasu ka aruite ikimasu ka?

6. I shall take my car (go in my car).
   Watakushi wa watakushi no jidōsha de ikimasu.

7. How many people will go with you?
   Nannin anata to issho ni ikimasu ka?

8. Four people will go—you, my younger sister, my older brother, and my friend.
   Yonin ikimasu. Anata to watakushi no imōto to ani to watakushi no tomodachi desu.

LESSON 33 EXERCISES

1. Are you going to Hakone next Saturday?
   Anata wa tsugi no Doyōbi ni Hakone e ikimasu ka?

2. Yes, I shall go.
   Hai, ikimasu.

3. How long (until when) will you be there?
   Anata wa itsu made soko ni imasu ka?

4. If the weather is good, I will be there from Saturday afternoon to Monday evening.
   Yoi tenki nara watakushi wa Doyōbi no gogo kara Getsuyōbi no yūgata made imasu.

5. Where will you be in Hakone?
   Anata wa Hakone no doko ni imasu ka?

6. I will probably be in the Hakone Hotel.
   Watakushi wa tabun Hakone hoteru ni imashō.

7. Isn't that hotel very expensive?
   Sono hoteru wa taihen takaku arimasen ka?

8. If it is too expensive, I will go to my friend's house at Miyanoshita.
    Amari takai nara watakushi wa Miyanoshita no watakushi no tomodachi no ie ni ikimasu.

9. Whenever I go to Hakone, it always rains.
    Watakushi ga Hakone e iku to itsumo ame ga furimasu.

10. Then let's go to Nikko.
    Soredewa Nikkō e ikimashō.

LESSON 34 EXERCISES

1. Please give me the key to my room.
    Dōzo watakushi ni watakushi no heya no kagi o kudasai.

2. Is this your key?
    Kore ga anata no kagi desu ka?

3. No, that is not mine. Mine is in the box on the left.
    Iie, sore wa watakushi no dewa arimasen. Watakushi no wa hidari no hako no naka ni arimasu.

4. Oh, yes, I have forgotten. Please forgive me.
    Aa sō desu. Wasuremashita. Dōmo sumimasen.

5. Don't mention it.
    Dō itashimashite.

6. Will you eat dinner in your room?
    Anata wa bangohan o anata no heya de tabemasu ka?

7. I think so. If Mr. Smith is here at six o'clock, please bring dinner to my room. How much are these newspapers?
Sō omoimasu. Moshi Sumisu san ga rokuji ni koko e kuru nara dōzo bangohan o watakushi no heya e motte kite kudasai. Kono shimbun wa ikura desu ka?

8. Ten yen.
Jūen.

9. Thank you.
Arigatō gozaimasu.

10. Will you take a walk this evening?
Anata wa yūgata sampo shimasu ka?

11. No, I will go to bed early tonight. Please bring breakfast to my room at seven o'clock tomorrow morning.
Iie, watakushi wa komban hayaku yasumimasu. Dōzo ashita no asa asagohan o shichiji ni watakushi no heya e motte kite kudasai.

LESSON 35 EXERCISES

1. It has become late. Do you want to eat dinner?
Osoku narimashita. Anata wa bangohan o tabetai desu ka?

2. Yes, I want to eat dinner.
Hai, watakushi wa bangohan o tabetai desu.

3. Which do you desire, tempura or sukiyaki?
Tempura to sukiyaki to dochira ga hoshii desu ka?

4. Please bring me sukiyaki.
   Dōzo sukiyaki o motte kite kudasai.

5. Do you want to dance afterwards?
   Sorekara anata wa dansu o shitai desu ko?

6. No. I do not want to dance tonight. If it is good weather
   tomorrow, I want to go to Nikko. I want to go to bed
   early tonight.
   Iie, watakushi wa komban dansu o shitaku arimasen.
   Moshi ashita yoi tenki nara watakushi wa Nikkō e ikitai
   desu. Watakushi wa komban hayaku yasumitai desu.

7. Do you want to go with me in my car?
   Anata wa watakushi to issho ni watakushi no jidōsha
   de ikitai desu ka?

8. Yes, that's excellent. Thank you very much.
   Hai, kekkō desu. Dōmo arigatō gozaimasu.

9. If it is raining, let us go by train.
   Moshi ame ga furu nara kisha de ikimashō.

Answers for Reviews, Lessons 27 and 36

LESSON 27 REVIEW

This section contains Japanese answers for the Exercises for the Review in Lesson 27.

1. *Iie, sore wa densha dewa arimasen. Denwa desu.*

2. *Hai, sore wa jidōsha desu.*

3. *Iie, sore wa haizara desu.*

4. *Iie, sore wa chiisai ie dewa arimasen. Ōkii desu.*

5. *Iie, sore wa karuku wa arimasen. Omoi desu.*

6. *Hai, sono hito wa ojisan desu.*

7. *Iie, sore wa sumisu san no empitsu dewa arimasen. Sumisu san no mannenhitsu desu.*

8. *Iie, sono hon wa sumisu san no dewa arimasen. Jōnzu san no desu.*

9. *Hai, sono hito wa Nihonjin desu.*

10. *Iie, sono hito wa jōbu na otoko no hito dewa arimasen. Sono ko wa chiisai onna no ko desu.*

11. *Hai, ano fune wa chiisaku wa arimasen. Ōkii desu.*

12. *Ima wa fuyu desu.*

13. *Iie, yottsu no ringo ga sara no naka ni arimasen. Mittsu desu.*

14. *Iie, hikōki no naka ni futari no hito ga imasen. Hitori no hito ga imasu.*

15. *Hai, ki wa ie no mae ni arimasu.*

16. *Hai, onna no ko wa uchi ni imasen. Kyōkai ni yukimasu.*

17. *Hai, otoko no ko to onna no ko wa jidōsha no soba ni imasu.*

18. *Hai, hibachi to ozen wa dentō no shita ni arimasu.*

19. *Iie, anata wa nemasen. Anata wa tabemasu.*

20. *Hai, otoko no ko wa arukimasen.*

21. *Iie, sono hito wa kesa shimbun o yomimasen deshita.*

22. *Hai, anata wa sakuban mado o akemashita.*

23. *Iie, anata wa takusan bīru o nomimashita.*

24. *Iie, anata wa tegami o dōe san no okusan ni okurimasen. Anata wa jōnzu san no okusan ni sore o okurimasu.*

25. *Iie, sono basu wa atami e ikimasen. Sore wa Tōkyō e ikimasu.*

26. *Iie, tēburu no ue ni bōshi wa nanatsu arimasen. Futatsu arimasu.*

27. *Iie, anata wa suika o mittsu kaimasen deshita. Anata wa hitotsu kaimashita.*

28. *Iie, wa tabun samuku wa arimasen. Ashita wa tabun taihen atsui deshō.*

29. *Iie, watakushitachi wa tabun ashita umi e ikimasen. Ashita wa tabun taihen samui deshō.*

30. *Iie, ima hiruhan o tabemashō.*

31. *Iie, watakushi wa jidōsha de yama e ikimasen deshita. Watakushi wa jitensha de ikimashita.*

32. *Hai, sono bōto wa ki de tsukurimashita.*

33. *Iie, watakushi wa sono heya de furansugo o benkyō shite imasen. Watakushi wa Nihongo o benkyō shite imasu.*

34. *Iie, byōin no mae ni ki wa roppon arimasen. Sambon desu.*

35. *Iie, sannin no seito ga jitensha de gakkō e kimashita.*

36. *Hai, sono yonhon no ki wa byōin no ushiro ni arimasu.*

37. *Watakushi wa maiasa _____ ni okimasu.*

38. *Iie, sono kisha wa hiru ni demasen. Sore wa jūji jūgofun ni demasu.*

39. *Watakushi wa _____ ni yasumimasu.*

40. *Iie, watakushi wa hachiji kara goji made mainichi benkyō shimasen. Watakushi wa doyōbi no gogo to Nichiyobi ni yasumimasu.*

41. *Iie, yuki wa natsu ni wa furimasen.*

42. *Watakushi wa nichiyōbi no yoru kyōkai e ikimasu.*

43. *Iie, chiisai onna no ko wa ōkii otoko no ko yori ōkiku arimasen.*
    Ōkii otoko no ko wa chiisai onna no ko yori ōkii desu.

44. *Iie, migi no empitsu wa ichiban nagaku arimasen.*
    Mannaka no empitsu ga ichiban nagai desu.

45. *Migi no kimono ga ichiban takai desu.*

46. *Hidari no hō no jidōsha wa furui desu.*

LESSON 36 REVIEW

This section contains Japanese answers for the Exercises for the Review in Lesson 36.

REVIEW A

1. *Iie, anata wa Tōkyō kara Miyanoshita made kisha de iku koto ga dekimasen. Anata wa Tōkyō kara Odawara made kisha de iku koto ga dekimasu. Odawara kara Miyanoshita made densha de ikimasu.*

2. *Iie, kisha wa Odawara kara Tōkyō made ikimasen. (kisha wa) Fujisawa kara Odawara made ikimasu.*

3. *Iie, jidōsha wa Fujisawa e ikimasen. (jidōsha wa) Tōkyō e ikimasu.*

4. *Tōkyō kara Miyanoshita made kisha no hō ga hayaku ikimasu.*

5. *Fujisawa wa Yokohama o minami no hō ni arimasu.*

6. *Iie, Odawara wa Tōkyō no minami ni arimasu.*

7. *Mizuumi ni fune ga hitotsu arimasu.*

8. *Fujisan ga ichiban takai yama desu.*

9. *Anata ga Tōkyō o jidōsha de hiru ni deru to anata wa jūniji sanjū-gofun sugi ni Yokohama e tsukimasu. Fujisawa e wa ichiji ni tsukimasu. Odawara e wa ichiji gojuppun sugi ni tsukimasu. Miyanoshita e wa nijihan ni tsukimasu.*

10. *Odawara o gozen kuji ni kisha de deru to anata wa Tōkyō e jūji sanjū-kyūfun sugi ni tsukimasu.*

11. *Tōkyō kara Yokohama made jidosha e sanjū-gofun kakarimasu. Yokohama kara Fujisawa made nijū-gofun kakarimasu. Fujisawa kara Odawara made gojuppun kakarimasu. Odawara kara Miyanoshita made yonjuppun kakarimasu.*

12. *Tōkyō kara Yokohama made nijū-roku kiromētoru arimasu. Yokohama kara Fujisawa made nijū-ni kiromētoru arimasu. Fujisawa kara Odawara made sanjū-san kiromētoru arimasu. Odawara kara Miyanoshita made jūni kiromētoru arimasu.*

REVIEW B

Picture A

1. *Kinyōbi desu.*

2. *Jūnigatsu desu.*

3. *Jūji desu.*

4. *Tokei wa tēburu no ue ni arimasu.*

5. *Samui desu.*

6. *Yuki ga futte imasu.*

7. *Iie, asatte wa Christmas desu.*

8. *Iie, kesa wa samui desu.*

9. *Isu wa tēburu no mae ni arimasu.*

10. *Tēburu no hō ga mado no chikaku ni arimasu.*

Picture B

1. *Iie, sakuban wa yuki ga furimasen deshita.*

2. *Hai, nichiyōbi dewa arimasen deshita. Kinō wa kayōbi deshita.*

3. *Iie, ima wa niji desu.*

4. *Iie, hana wa ie no soto ni arimasu.*

5. *Kongetsu wa shichigatsu desu.*

6. *Kono heya ni tēburu ga hitotsu arimasu.*

7. *Iie, ashita wa taihen atsuku narimasu.*

8. *Iie, ano hito wa isu no tokoro e ikimasu.*

9. *Ima wa gogo desu.*

10. *Hai, ano hito wa shimbun o yomimasu.*

Picture C

1. *Ima wa gozen sanji desu.*

2. *Anata wa ima yasunde imasu.*

3. *Hai, anata wa kesa kyōkai e ikimashō.*

4. *Tsuki wa mado no migi ni arimasu.*

5. *Iie, kongetsu wa ichigatsu dewa arimasen. Jūgatsu desu.*

6. *Tēburu wa yonhon no ashi ga arimasu.*

7. *Iie, komban no tenki wa yoi desu.*

8. *Watakushi wa asahan o _____ ni tabemasu. Hiruhan wa _____ ni tabemasu. Bangohan wa _____ ni tabemasu.*

9. *Hako wa tēburu no migi ni arimasu.*

10. *Hai, hako wa ki de tsukurimashita.*

Picture D

1. *Iie, yuki wa futte imasen.*

2. *Iie, sakuban wa suzushii deshita.*

3. *Kinō wa getsuyōbi deshita.*

4. *Iie, anata wa kono heya dewa tabemasen. Kono heya de nemasu.*

5. *Anata wa yojikan hatarakimasu.*

6. *Watakushi wa maiasa _____ ni okimasu.*

7. *Gogatsu ga shigatsu yori nagai desu.*

8. *Dentō wa tēburu no ue ni arimasu. Tēburu wa heya no naka ni arimasu. Isu wa tēburu no mae ni arimasu. Shindai wa mado no soba ni arimasu.*

9. *Iie, anata wa ima yasunde imasen.*

10. *Heya no naka ni hito wa imasen.*

REVIEW C

Part 1

1. *Futari no otoko no hito ga nonde imasu.*

2. *Ano hitotachi wa tsumetai bīru o nonde imasu.*

3. *Otoko no hito wa ki no shita de yasunde imasu.*

4. *Ano hito wa machi e itte bīru o nomimasu.*

5.   *Iie, ano hitotachi wa tenki ga warui to hatarakimasen.*

6.   *Iie, ano hitotachi wa jitensha de uchi e kaerimasen.*
     Ano hitotachi wa uche e aruite kaerimasu.

7.   *Ano hitotachi wa yukkuri aruite imasu.*

8.   *Ano hitotachi wa hiruhan o tabete imasu.*

9.   *Iie, ano hito wa tomodachi e tegami o kaite imasen.*
     Ano hito wa tabete imasu.

10.   *Hai, watakushi wa tsumetai bīru ga taihen suki desu.*

Part 2

1.   *Sannin no seito wa gakkō e aruite kimashita.*

2.   *Seito wa minna jidōsha de gakkō e kimasen deshita.*

3.   *Onna no ko wa otoko no ko yori chiisai desu.*

4.   *Otoko no ko wa hidari no te ni ringo o motte imasu.*

5.   *Otoko no ko wa migi no te ni hon o motte imasu.*

6.   *Seito no bōshi wa seito no atama no ue ni arimasu.*

7.   *Seito wa gakkō de eigo o benkyō shimasu.*

8. *Watakushi wa kono heya de Nihongo o benkyō shimasu.*

9. *Iie, watakushi wa Nihongo o yomu koto to kaku koto ga dekimasen.*

10. *Iie, watakushi wa maiban benkyō o shimasen. Watakushi wa _____ no yoru benkyō shimasu.*

APPENDIX I

Japanese Writing System and Pronunciation

Written language came to Japan in the third century CE, when the Chinese ideographic script, or *kanji* was adopted. While the acquisition of a written language was a major boon to Japanese culture, the transition was a difficult one for many reasons. The primary challenge emerged from the fact that Chinese is a monosyllabic, inflected language, meaning that a single syllable can have many different meanings depending on how it is spoken. Japanese, like English, is a polysyllabic language in which inflection does not affect meaning. In addition, kanji ideograms are very complex, some being comprised of twenty strokes or more with clear standards for both stroke form and stroke order.

Because of these challenges, the written language of Japan evolved into a mixture of forms, each with a specific role in written expression. These forms are:

Kanji: The Japanese form of the Chinese written language described above. Ideograms number in the thousands, and each one is linked to an idea rather than a sound. Kanji is most often used to express place names, people's names and many other nouns, along with verb and adjective stems.

Katakaná: An angular script, katakaná is a phonetic syllabary, comprised of 46 basic characters. Each character corresponds to one sound in the Japanese language. It is most often used to express non-Japanese names, words borrowed from other languages, names of companies, and recent entrants into the Japanese language.

Hiraganá: A smoother, more flowing script, hiragana is a phonetic syllabary, like katakaná. There are 46 basic characters, each corresponding to a sound. Hiraganá shares most of the rules of katakaná and is the first writing system taught in Japanese schools. Therefore, most children's books are written in hiraganá. As students learn kanji, difficult or complex ideograms may be supplemented by hiraganá pronunciations in textbooks. Hiraganá is most often used to express simple words, verb conjugations, and particles of speech.

Katakaná and hiraganá are known collectively as *kaná*, and evolved out of the kanji system roughly five centuries after its adoption.

Romaji: Romaji is the "Romanized" version of Japanese, or the use of the Latin alphabet with which we are all familiar to write out Japanese sounds. There are numerous systems used to make Japanese easier for Westerners to learn, including the *Kunrei-Shiki* and the *Nippon* systems. By far the most popular is the Hepburn system, which is the one used in this text. While romaji will be invaluable in early study, and can be essential to business travelers or others who wish only to "get around" in Japan, students should not become too reliant on it. It is not a perfect system, and obscures some connections between words in which the same kana characters are used. In Japan, romaji appears in the popular press and in tourist information. Most Japanese have a working knowledge of romaji, can spell their names, sound out romjai words, etc.

The mix of these systems can be confusing for the beginning student, but it adds to the richness of the Japanese written language. While the two kana systems cannot be mixed in a single word, there is otherwise a great deal of freedom of expression provided by blending systems. Experienced students and native speakers will often blend systems to suit their purpose and audience.

In the first of the following tables are given the *katakana* characters arranged in the Japanese order of the *go-jū-on* 五十音 "the fifty sounds." Under each *katakana* is given the corresponding *hiragana*, and under that the equivalent in roman letters.

Katakaná and Hiraganá

Table I

ワ	ラ	ヤ	マ	ハ	ナ	タ	サ	カ	ア
わ	ら	や	ま	は	な	た	さ	か	あ
wa	ra	ya	ma	ha	na	ta	sa	ka	a
ヰ	リ	イ	ミ	ヒ	ニ	チ	シ	キ	イ
ゐ	り	い	み	ひ	に	ち	し	き	い
i	ri	i	mi	hi	ni	chi	shi	ki	i
ウ	ル	ユ	ム	フ	ヌ	ツ	ス	ク	ウ
う	る	ゆ	む	ふ	ぬ	つ	す	く	う
u	ru	yu	mu	fu	nu	tsu	su	ku	u
エ	レ	エ	メ	ヘ	ネ	テ	セ	ケ	エ
ゑ	れ	え	め	へ	ね	て	せ	け	え
e	re	e	me	he	ne	te	se	ke	e

ン	ヲ	ロ	ヨ	モ	ホ	ノ	ト	ソ	コ	オ
ん	を	ろ	よ	も	ほ	の	と	そ	こ	お
n	wo	ro	yo	mo	ho	no	to	so	ko	o

By putting two small marks or a small circle on the right side of the upper part of certain syllables; their sound is modified.

The two small marks are called *nigori* 濁, and the small circle is called *maru* 丸 or *handaku* 半濁.

Table II

ヴァ ア va	バ ば pa	バ ば ba	ダ だ da	ザ ざ za	ガ が ga
ヴィ イ vi	ピ び p	ビ び bi	ヂ ぢ ji	ジ じ ji	ギ ぎ gi
ヴ vu	プ ぶ pu	ブ ぶ bu	ヅ づ zu	ズ ず zu	グ ぐ gu
ヴェ エ ve	ペ ぺ pe	ベ べ be	デ で de	ゼ ぜ ze	ゲ げ ge
ヴォ オ vo	ポ ぼ po	ボ ぼ bo	ド ど do	ゾ ぞ zo	ゴ ご go

N. B. The separate column on the left includes four combinations of characters representing the sounds of the consonant *v* with the four vowels *a, i, e,* and *o,* and one single character to represent the sound of *v* and *u,* all of which are used only to write foreign words.

In writing words of foreign derivation, the sound of **di,** as in the word *dictation,* may be represented by the symbol ヂ or ディ.

    birudingu ビルヂング or ビルディング   building

By the combination of certain syllables with *ya* ヤ, *yu* ユ, and *yo* ヨ, other sounds are obtained. In this case the characters corresponding to *ya*, *yu*, and *yo* are written in a smaller size than the characters with which they are combined.

Table III

リャ りゃ rya	ミャ みゃ mya	ヒャ ひゃ hya	ニャ にゃ nya	チャ ちゃ cha	シャ しゃ sha	キャ きゃ kya
リュ りゅ ryu	ミュ みゅ myu	ヒュ ひゅ hyu	ニュ にゅ nyu	チュ ちゅ chu	シュ しゅ shu	キュ きゅ kyu
リョ りょ ryo	ミョ みょ myo	ヒョ ひょ hyo	ニョ にょ nyo	チョ ちょ cho	ショ しょ sho	キョ きょ kyo
ピャ びゃ pya	ビャ びゃ bya	ヂャ ぢゃ ja	ジャ じゃ ja	ギャ ぎゃ gya		
ピュ びゅ pyu	ビュ びゅ byu	ヂュ ぢゅ ju	ジュ じゅ ju	ギュ ぎゅ gyu		
ピョ びょ pyo	ビョ びょ byo	ヂョ ぢょ jo	ジョ じょ jo	ギョ ぎょ gyo		

Note that all the Japanese characters transliterated with roman letters and containing *y* in the body of the syllable have diphthongal sounds.

Short Vowels

A, a   is pronounced as **a** in *father.*
E, e   as in the first syllable of the words *enamel, enemy, edge, melody.*
I, i   as e in *me, be.*
O, o   as in *oasis, opinion, original.*
U, u   as in *put, push, pull, full.*

The *u* of the syllable *su* is almost silent when followed by a syllable beginning with *k,* and the *u* of the syllable *ku* is, in certain words, almost silent when followed by a syllable beginning with *s.*

U is almost silent also in the verbal suffix *masu* マス, as in *tabemasu (tabemas')* 食べマス I eat, *ikimasu (ikimas')* 行キマス I go.

sukoshi (s'koshi) 少シ little   *suki*   *(s'ki)* 好キ I like
takusan (tak'san) 沢山 much   *okusan (ok'san)* 奥サン Madam

In certain words, and invariably in the suffix *máshita* マシタ, also the vowel *i* is almost silent, as in the following examples:

shitá (sh'ta) 下 *under*

ikimáshita 行キマシタ I went

mimáshita 見マシタ I saw

The graphic accent placed on one of the vowels of each of the above words given as phonetic examples indicates the force of utterance to be laid on their stressed syllables.

Long Vowels

The long vowels are characterized by a line placed above them.
Ā, ā   as in *park, lark, spark.*
Ē, ē   as the sound of a in *ape, fame, same* or *ay* in *day, may, say.*
Ō, ō   as in *so, old,* and as *oa* in *oats, oath.*
Ū, ū   as *oo* in *boom, soon, broom, spoon.*
The long vowel *e* is often written *ei.*

The long sound of *i* (pron. ee, as in beer) is generally written *ii.*

okāsan	オ母サン	mother	*ōkii*	大キイ	big, large
obāsan	オバアサン	grandmother	*kōsan*	降参	surrender
nēsan	姉サン	elder sister	*ureshii*	ウレシイ	glad, happy
kēsan	ケーサン	paper weight	*kanashii*	カナシイ	sad
eikō	栄光	glory	*joyū*	女優	actress
heitai	兵隊	soldier	*kūshū*	空襲	air raid
kōhei	公平	impartiality	*sabishii*	淋シイ	lonesome
kōkei	光景	a scene	*niisan*	兄サン	elder brother
sōkei	総計	total amount			

Note that it is essential to distinguish long from short vowel sounds, if one wishes to speak the Japanese language intelligibly. Many words written with short vowels have a different meaning when written with long vowels.

koshi	腰	the waist	*kōshi*	孝子	dutiful child
kōsei	個性	personality	*kōsei*	校正	proofreading
suji	筋	muscle	*sūji*	数字	a numeral, a figure
bōshi	拇指	thumb	*bōshi*	帽子	hat
kuki	茎	a stalk	*kūki*	空気	air
kosui	湖水	a lake	*kōsui*	香水	perfume
kuro	黒	black	*kurō*	苦労	suffering
tōru	取ル	to take	*tōru*	通ル	to go through
toshi	年	year	*tōshi*	投資	investment

When writing Japanese with *kana,* the sound of the long vowel *a* may be represented by the symbol ア, placed after the character containing the long vowel, as in the following examples:

> *obāsan* オバアサン grandmother
> *okāsan* オカアサン mother

The sound of the long vowel *o* may be represented in five ways, as shown in Table IV and Table V, and the long vowel *u* in two ways, as given in Table VIII.

The different ways of representing the sound of the long vowels *o* and *u* are indiscriminately used by the Japanese, both in writing and in printing. However, to avoid confusion, the sound of the long vowel *o* and *u* has been represented in this book in one way only, as given in the upper division of each of the following tables.

Katakaná

Table IV

rō	yō	mō	pō	bō	hō	nō	dō	tō	zō	sō	gō	kō	ō
ロオ	ヨオ	モオ	ボオ	ボオ	ホオ	ノオ	ドオ	トオ	ゾオ	ソオ	ゴオ	コオ	オオ
ロウ	ヨウ	モウ	ボウ	ボウ	ホウ	ノウ	ドウ	トウ	ゾウ	ソウ	ゴウ	コウ	オウ
ラウ	ヤウ	マウ	バウ	バウ	ハウ	ナウ	ダウ	タウ	ザウ	サウ	ガウ	カウ	アウ
ラフ	ヤフ	マフ	バフ	バフ	ハフ	ナフ	ダフ	タフ	ザフ	サフ	ガフ	カフ	アフ
ロフ	ヨフ	モフ	ボフ	ボフ	ホフ	ノフ	ドフ	トフ	ゾフ	ソフ	ゴフ	コフ	オフ

OBSOLETE SPELLING

ō
ヲウ
ワウ
ワフ
ヲフ

Hiraganá

Table V

rō	yō	mō	pō	bō	hō	nō	dō	tō	zō	sō	gō	kō	ō
ろお	よお	もお	ぼお	ぼお	ほお	のお	どお	とお	ぞお	そお	ごお	こお	おお
ろう	よう	もう	ぼう	ぼう	ほう	のう	どう	とう	ぞう	そう	ごう	こう	おう
らう	やう	まう	ばう	ばう	はう	なう	だう	たう	ざう	さう	がう	かう	あう
らふ	やふ	まふ	ばふ	ばふ	はふ	なふ	だふ	たふ	ざふ	さふ	がふ	かふ	あふ
ろふ	よふ	もふ	ぼふ	ぼふ	ほふ	のふ	どふ	とふ	ぞふ	そふ	ごふ	こふ	おふ

OBSOLETE SPELLING

ō
をう
わう
わふ
をふ

Katakaná

Table VI

ryō	myō	pyō	byō	hyō	nyō	chō	shō	gyō	kyō	jō		jō
リョウ	ミョウ	ピョウ	ビョウ	ヒョウ	ニョウ	チョウ	ショウ	ギョウ	キョウ	ジョウ		チョウ
リャウ	ミャウ	ピャウ	ビャウ	ヒャウ	ニャウ	チャウ	シャウ	ギャウ	キャウ	ジャウ		チャウ
レウ	メウ	ペウ	ベウ	ヘウ	ネウ	テウ	セウ	ゲウ	ケウ	ゼウ		デウ
レフ	ミフ	ペフ	ベフ	ヘフ	ネフ	テフ	セフ	ゲフ	ケフ	ゼフ		デフ

OBSOLETE SPELLING

Hiraganá

Table VII

ryō	myō	pyō	byō	hyō	nyō	chō	shō	gyo	kyō	jō		jō
りょう	みょう	ぴょう	びょう	ひょう	にょう	ちょう	しょう	ぎょう	きょう	じょう		ぢょう
りゃう	みゃう	ぴゃう	びゃう	ひゃう	にゃう	ちゃう	しゃう	ぎゃう	きゃう	じゃう		ぢゃう
れう	めう	ぺう	べう	べう	ねう	てう	せう	げう	けう	ぜう		でう
れふ	みふ	ぺふ	べふ	へふ	ねふ	てふ	せふ	げふ	けふ	ぜふ		でふ

OBSOLETE SPELLING

Japanese for Beginners

Table VIII

ryū	myū	pyū	byū	hyū	nyū	jū	chū	jū	shū	gyū	kyū	yū
リュウ	ミュウ	ピュウ	ビュウ	ヒュウ	ニュウ	ヂュウ	チュウ	ジュウ	シュウ	ギュウ	キュウ	ユウ
リフ	ミフ	ピフ	ビフ	ヒフ	ニフ	ヂフ	チフ	ジフ	シフ	ギフ	キフ	ユフ

The sound of all long vowels may also be represented, when writing in *kana*, by a bar placed immediately after the syllable containing the long vowel, especially when writing certain words of foreign derivation, as shown in the following examples:

bīru	ビール	beer
erebētā	エレベーター	elevator
kōhī	コーヒー	coffee
sŭtēshon	ステーション	station
taipŭraitā	タイプライター	typewriter
tēburu	テーブル	table

Note that words of foreign derivation generally maintain the accent upon the syllable corresponding to the one stressed in the original foreign word.

When a *kana* character is repeated in succession in the same word, the duplicated character is represented by the symbol ヽ.

háha ハヽ mother   **chíchi** チヽ father

When writing Japanese in horizontal lines, a word written in *kana* may be regularly repeated with syllabic characters, as for instance *iró-iró* イロイロ *various*, *kutá-kutá* クタ クタ *worn out*, but when writing Japanese in vertical lines, the repetition is indicated by a long mark resembling the character 〱 (ku) of the *hiragana* syllabary, as shown on the right side of this explanation.

The symbol ヽ takes the *nigori* when it is used to indicate that the sound of the duplicated character is altered according to Table III.

Ex: *kagamí* カヾミ mirror   *kogotó* コヾト a scolding

Also the symbol used to indicate the repetition of ト ク
a word takes the *nigori* when the sound of the first キ ニ
character of the duplicated word is altered according to
Table III. The words vertically written on the right 〳〵 〳〵
of this explanation correspond to the ones given below.

kuníguni クニグニ countries   *tokidoki* トキドキ now and then

The repetition of a *kanji* is indicated by the symbol 々.

iró-iró 色々 various   *tabi-tabi* 度々 often

Consonants

The consonants *b, d, j, k, m, n, p,* and *t,* are pronounced as
they are in English.

G is always pronounced hard as in *garland.* Ex. *gakú* 額 framed
picture, *géki* 劇 a drama, *gímu* 義務 duty, *gógo* 午後 afternoon.
When *g* is in the body of a word, it is generally pronounced as if
it were preceded by a faint sound of n. Ex. *kagó* (*ka_ngo*) 籠 cage,
kagamí (*ka_ngami*) 鏡 mirror.

F is pronounced with the two lips a little apart, and one's lower
and upper teeth almost in contact, not with the lower lip and the
upper teeth as Western people pronounce it.

H is always pronounced aspirated as in *hope.*

The symbol ン, corresponding to the sound of *n,* is pronounced
m before *b, p* and *m.*

シンブン *shimbún* newspaper ワンパクナ *wámpaku-na* naughty
センモンカ *semmonká* specialist ホンモノ *hommonó* genuine article

R is not pronounced as distinctly as it is in English; it approaches
the sound of l, but until one hears it from a Japanese, it is better
not to try to pronounce it differently from the natural way one is
accustomed to.

The sound of l does not exist in the Japanese language, and when
foreign words containing this consonant are to be written with *kana*
characters, the r symbols are used.

Labrador *Rabŭradorú* ラブラドル lamp   *rámpu* ランプ
London   *Róndon* ロンドン lemonade *remonédo* レモネード

S before a vowel, is always pronounced as in *salmon, self, solar.*

Sh is pronounced as in *shaft, sheep.*

Ch is pronounced as in *cherry, chief, choice.*

The syllable *wa* is pronounced as in *waft,* and the syllable *wo,* which is used to indicate the accusative case, is pronounced as **wo** in *worship,* when it follows a word ending in *n,* but when it follows a word ending in a vowel, the *w* is almost silent.

wakái	ワカイ	young	*waraú*	ワラウ	to laugh
hon wo	ホンヲ	the book	*umá wo*	ウマヲ	the horse

Y is pronounced as in English in the words *yacht, yell, yonder, you.* When **y** is preceded by **i,** both letters should be pronounced distinctly to avoid mistaking their combined sound for that of some of the diphtongs given in Table IV.

biyóin	美ヒ容ヶ院ヶ	beauty parlour	*byóin*	病ビヶ院ヶ	hospital
kíyo	器ヰ用ヶ	skillful	*kyó*	今日(キョウ)	to-day

Z is pronounced as in *zeal, zodiac, zone.*

Double Consonants

Care must be taken to distinguish single from double consonants, as many words that have single consonants change meaning when these are pronounced double. The double consonants are pronounced in Japanese as they are in **Italian,** that is, they are stressed by holding for a moment the **vocal organs** in the position required to pronounce them.

kóka	古ョ歌ヵ	an old song	*kokká*	国ヶ歌ヵ	national anthem
isó	磯ヶ	beach	*issó*	一ヶ層ヶ	more
sóto	外ヰ	outside	*sottó*	ソット	softly
tokú	徳ヶ	virtue	*tokkú*	トック	already
hikakú	比ヒ較ヶ	comparison	*hikkáku*	引ヶ掻ヵク	to scratch

The small *katakaná* on the right side of the above *kanji* indicate the pronunciation of the latter.

The phonetic syllables attached to ideograms, whether written with *katakaná* or *hiraganá,* are called *furiganá* 振ヶ仮ヵ名ナ. Use of furiganá was once frowned upon in Japan. But today, in the age of the Internet and international commerce, furiganá is viewed as a "necessary evil," since, essentially the writer is using the same sound twice.

Katakaná and *hiraganá* cannot be mixed in the same composition, so that the *furiganá* must be written with the characters of the same syllabary used with the ideograms.

The double consonants are indicated by having the affected character preceded by a small ツ (*tsu*), as shown in the above five words on the right.

The double pronunciation of **ch** is represented in roman characters by *tch* and in *kaná* characters by ツ placed before the affected syllable.

kotchí	コッチ	here	*dótchi*	ドッチ	which
atchí	アッチ	there	*mátchi*	マッチ	matches

Accentuation

Some of the early studies of the Japanese language expressed the view that the syllables of Japanese words bear scarcely any accentuation. This error concerning Japanese accentuation has been carried over into later studies, mainly because of inadequate research into this important aspect of the language.

The fact is that syllabic stresses vary in any words containing two or more syllables, no matter what the language may be.

If Japanese words are not correctly accented, they sound as oddly foreign to Japanese ears as, say, the English language sounds to English ears when spoken by French students who may tend to stress the last syllables of English words according to French usage.

The correct stress on Japanese syllables is the more important in that the Japanese language contains numerous words which, although spelled with the same letters, have different meaning according to the position of the stressed syllable.

The examples given below, which represent only a very small number of words spelled with the same letters but having different meaning according to the position of their stressed syllable, will demonstrate how necessary it is to know the right accentuation of Japanese words.

ása	朝	morning	*asá*	麻	flax, hemp
haná	花	flower	*hána*	端	the outset, beginning
hashí	橋	a bridge	*háshi*	箸	chopsticks
ippái	いっぱい	full, up to the brim	*íppai*	一杯	one cupful
kagú	嗅ぐ	to smell	*kágu*	家具	furniture
karasu	枯らす	to let wither	*kárasu*	烏	a crow
kashí	貸し	loan	*káshi*	樫	oak tree

kaú	買う	to buy	káu	飼う	to keep (animals)
kiji	雉子	a pheasant	kiji	記事	article (of newspaper)
kirú	着る	to wear put on	kíru	切る	to cut
nashi	梨	a pear	náshi	無し	without
magó	孫	grandchild	mágd	馬子	pack-horseman
omoi	重い	heavy	omói	思い	emotion, feeling
séki	席	seat, pew	seki	咳	cough
shimai	姉妹	sisters	shimai	仕舞	end, close
tátsv	立つ	to stand up	tatsú	竜	dragon
új i	氏	family stock	uji	蛆	larva
yói	良い	good	yoi	宵	early evening

To provide the student with the essential approach to correct pronunciation, the authors have had a graphic accent printed on the stressed syllable of the Japanese words given throughout the book.

This new and unique feature will prove to be of great benefit to the student, as he will be able, from the very beginning of his study, and without mental effort, to pronounce the words he gradually learns, correctly and intelligibly to Japanese ears.

Romanization of the Language

There are three systems of romanization of the Japanese language. Of the three, however, the Hepburn system is by far the most widley used, both in Japan as well as abroad, for which reason it has been adopted by this volume.

Below, the syllables of the three systems that are differently spelled are given for comparison:

Hepburn Spelling	Nippon Spelling	Kunrei Spelling
cha	tya	tya
chi	ti	ti
chu	tyu	tyu
cho	tyo	tyo
fu	hu	hu
ja	dya	zya
ji	di	zi
ju	dyu	zyu
jo	dyo	zyo
sha	sya	sya
shi	si	si
shu	syu	syu
sho	syo	syo
tsu	tu	tu

VOCABULARY

ENGLISH-JAPANESE VOCABULARY

The numerals in parentheses indicate the lessons in which the words are introduced. Words not followed by numerals have been added to those appearing in the lesson.

A

abdomen (18) .... *hara*

actress .... *jyoyū*

address (on a letter) ... *atena*

after (24) .... *sugi*

afternoon (24) .... *gogo*

afterwards (22) ...... *sorekara*

again .... *mata*

airplane (13) .... *hikōki*

alcove (18) .... *tokonoma*

all (23) .... *minna*

all right .... *daijōbu*

alone .... *hitori de*

already (30) .... *mō*

also (26) .... *mo*

always .... *itsumo*

am (1) .... *desu*

A.M. (24) .... *gozen*

America (4) .... *Amerika*

American (6) ..... *Amerikajin*

am not (2) ... *dewa arimasen*

among (26) .... *no naka*

and (13) .... *to*

ankle (18) .... *ashikubi*

anxiety .... *shimpai*

apple (13) .... *ringo*

April (26) .... *Shigatsu*

are (1) .... *desu*

are not (2) ..... *dewa arimasen*

arm (18) .... *ude*

armed forces .... *guntai*

arrive (15) .... *tsuku*

as far as (24) .... *made*

ashtray .... *haizara*

at (10) .... *ni*

at (22) .... *de*

at once (33) .... *sugu*

August (26) .... *Hachigatsu*

automobile (5) .... *jidōsha*

autumn (5) .... *aki*

B

baby (4) .... *akambō*

bad (4) .... *warui*

bag, traveling (1) .... *kaban*

bamboo .... *take*

bank (for money) .... *ginkō*

barber .... *tokoya*

barracks .... *heisha*

bath .... *furo*

beautiful (3) .... *utsukushii*

become (30) .... *naru*

bed (western style)
(10) .... *shindai*

bed (Japanese style) ... *futon*

before (24) .... *mae*

best (26) .... *ichiban ii,
ichiban yoi*

between (10) .... *aida*

big (3) .... *ōkii*

bicycle (5) .... *jitensha*

bird (11) .... *tori*

black (3) .... *kuroi*

blossom, cherry (9) ..... *sakura*

blue (4) .... *aoi*

boat (13) .... *fune*

body (18) .... karada

boiler (9) .... kama

book (1) .... hon

bookcase .... hombako

bookstore (22) .... honya

boots, long (15) ..... nagagutsu

bothersome .... jama (na)

bottom (10) .... shita

bowl, rice (9) .... chawan

box (1) .... hako

boxing .... kentō

brazier, fire (15) ...... hibachi

bread (13) .... pan

breakfast (24) .... asagohan
(asahan)

breast (18) .... mune

brick (29) .... renga

bridge .... hashi

briefcase (1) .... kaban

broad (3) .... hiroi

broom (9) .... hōki

bucket (15) .... baketsu

build (29) .... tateru

building .... tatemono

bundle (12) .... tsutsumi

busy .... isogashii

butter (13) .... bata

buy (16) .... kau

C

camera (4) .... shashinki

cake (19) .... okashi

candy .... ame

cap (1) .... bōshi

captain (30) .... taii

car (auto) (15) .... jidōsha

carry .... motte iku

cat (2) .... neko

ceiling (8) .... tenjō

certainly .... mochiron

chair (1) .... isu

charming .... kawaii

cheap (4) .... *yasui*

cheek (18) .... *hoho*

chest (body) (18) .... *mune*

chest of drawers (11) ..*tansu*

child (4) .... *kodomo (ko)*

chin (18) .... *ago*

China (6) .... *Chūgoku*

Chinese (language) (6) .... *Chūgokugo*

Chinese (native) (6) .... *Chūgokujin*

chopsticks (9) .... *hashi*

church .... *kyōkai*

city .... *shi*

clean (6) .... *kirei*

clever (6) .... *rikō (na)*

clogs, wooden (15) .... *geta*

close (verb) (16) ...... *shimeru*

closet (13) .... *todana*

clumsy .... *heta (na)*

cold (in head) .... *kaze*

cold (weather) (7) ...... *samui*

college .... *daigaku*

comb (9) .... *kushi*

come (14) .... *kuru*

come out (24) .... *deru*

cooked rice (21) .... *gohan*

cool (weather) (7) .... *suzushii*

corner (inside) .... *sumi*

corner (outside) .... *kado*

cost .... *kakaru*

country (rural area) ... *inaka*

crab .... *kani*

curtain, shop (15) ...... *noren*

cushion (18) .... *zabuton*

cute .... *kawaii*

cutting board .... *manaita*

D

dance (35) .... *dansu; odori*

daughter .... *musume*

day (25) .... *hi*

day (in compound)
(25) .... *nichi*

day after tomorrow
(21) .... *asatte*

December (26) ..... *Jūnigatsu*

delicious .... *oishii*

depart (24) .... *deru*

desirous of having
(35) .... *hoshii*

desk (1) .... *tsukue*

detour .... *mawari michi*

dictionary (29) .... *jibiki*

difficult (7) .... *muzukashii*

dinner (evening meal)
(22) .... *bangohan*

direction (26) .... *hō*

dish (13) .... *sara*

displeasing .... *kirai (na)*

distant .... *tōi*

do (21) .... *suru*

doctor (9) .... *isha*

dog (2) .... *inu*

door (8) .... *to*

door, heavy paper
(18) .... *fusuma*

door, light paper
(18) .... *shoji*

downtown .... *shitamachi*

drama (play) .... *shibai*

draw (14) .... *kaku*

drawing (8) .... *e*

drink (14) .... *nomu*

drugstore .... *kusuriya*

drum, hand (15) ..... *tsuzumi*

E

ear (18) .... *mimi*

early (adjective) .... *hayai*

early (adverb) (29) ..... *hayaku*

earthquake .... *jishin*

east (36) .... *higashi*

easy (7) .... *yasashii*

eat (14) .... *taberu*

egg .... *tamago*

eight (20; 23) .... *yattsu; hachi*

eight hundred (23) .... *happyaku*

electric light (8) .... *dentō*

electric train (24) ..... *densha*

eleven (23) .... *jūichi*

England (6) .... *Igirisu*

English (lang.) (6) .... *Eigo*

Englishman (6) .... *Igirisujin*

enjoyable .... *tanoshii*

enlisted man .... *kashisotsu*

entertaining (6) .... *omoshiroi*

entrance .... *iriguchi*

envelope (12) .... *fūtō*

evening (8) .... *ban*

evening, last (15) ..... *sakuban*

evening, toward (8) .... *yūgata*

every (prefix) (25) .... *mai*

everybody .... *minna*

every day .... *mainichi*

everything (23) .... *minna*

excellent .... *kekkō*

exit .... *deguchi*

expensive (4) .... *takai*

express train .... *kyūkō*

eye (18) .... *me*

F

face (18) .... *kao*

factory .... *kōba*

fairly (30) .... *kanari*

fall (rain or snow) (verb) (33) .... *turu*

falsehood .... *uso*

fan, folding (15) .... *sensu*

fan, non-folding (15) .... *uchiwa*

far .... *tōi*

fast (adjective) .... *hayai*

fast (adverb) (29) ..... *hayaku*

father (12) .... *otōsan*

father (the speaker's) (19) .... chichi

February (26) .... Nigatsu

female (4) .... onna

finally (30) .... tōtō

fine (excellent) .... kekkō

fine looking (6) ..... kirei (na)

fire station .... shōbōsho

first time, for the (15) .... hajimete

fish (3) .... sakana

five (20; 23) .... itsutsu: go

five hundred (23) ..... gohyaku

fix (34) .... naosu

flag (4) .... hata

flat objects, word used in counting (23) .... mai

floor (8) .... yuka

floor, matted (18) ...... tatami

flower (3) .... hana

flute (15) .... fue

fog .... kiri

fond (of) .... suki

food .... tabemono

fool .... baka

foot (18) .... ashi

forehead (18) .... hitai

forenoon (24) .... gozen

forget (16) .... wasureru

forty (23) .... shijū or yonjū

fountain pen (2) .... mannenhitsu

four (20; 23) .... yottsu; shi or yon

four hundred (23) .... yonhyaku

fresh (3) .... atarashii

Friday (25) .... Kinyōbi

friend (14) .... tomodachi

from (24) .... kara

front (10) .... mae

fruit .... kudamono

Fuji, Mt. (9) .... Fujisan

G

gate .... *mon*

glass, drinking (13) ..... *koppu*

get (become) (30) .... *naru*

get up (25) .... *okiru*

give (to someone except the
speaker) (19) .... *ageru*

go (14) .... *iku; yuku*

good (4) .... *ii; yoi*

good at (6) ....*jōzu (na)*

go out (24) .... *deru; dekakeru*

go to bed (25) .... *yasumu*

grapes .... *budō*

green (4) .... *midori*

guide .... *annai*

H

hair (on the head)
(18) .... *kami*

half .... *hambun*

half past (24) .... *han*

hand (11) .... *te*

happy .... *kōfuku*

hat (1) .... *bōshi*

have (32) .... *motsu*

head (18) .... *atama*

healthy (6) ... *genki; jōbu (na)*

hear (22) .... *kiku*

heavy (3) .... *omoi*

here (11) .... *koko*

high (4) .... *takai*

high-spirited .... *genki (na)*

hold (32) .... *motsu*

home (12) .... *uchi*

horse (12) .... *uma*

hospital .... *byōin*

hot (weather) (7) .... *atsui*

hotel (Japanese style) ... *ryokan*

hour (24) ....*jikan*

house (3) .... *ie*

how many? (20) .... *ikutsu*

how many minutes? ... *nampun*

hurry (verb) (17) .... *isogu*

I

I (4) .... *watakushi, wata'shi*

ice .... *kōri*

if (33) .... *moshi; nara*

immediately .... *sugu*

important .... *taisetsu (na)*

in (10) .... *ni*

in (22) .... *de*

indeed (35) .... *dōmo*

inexpensive (4) .... *yasui*

inside (10) .... *naka*

intelligent (6) .... *rikō (na)*

interesting (6) ...... *omoshiroi*

is (1) .... *aru, desu, iru*

island .... *shima*

is not (2) ..... *dewa arimasen*

J

January (26) .... *Ichigatsu*

Japan (6) ..... *Nihon; Nippon*

Japanese (language) (6) .... *Nihongo; Nippongo*

Japanese (6) .... *Nihonjin; Nipponjin*

Japanese meat or fish deep fry (35) .... *tempura*

Japanese meat and vegetable dish (35) .... *sukiyaki*

job .... *shigoto*

joke .... *jōdan*

July (26) .... *Shichigatsu*

June (26) .... *Rokugatsu*

K

kettle (9) .... *kama*

kettle, tea (9) .... *dobin*

key (13) .... *kagi*

kilometer .... *kiromētoru*

kind (adj.) ..... *shinsetsu (na)*

kitchen (20) .... *daidokoro*

L

lacquerware .... *nurimono*

lake .... *mizuumi*

lantern, Japanese paper (9) .... *chōchin* lantern, stone or metal (9) .... *tōrō*

large (3) .... *ōkii*

large (in area) (3) .... *hiroi*

last evening (15) .... *sakuban*

late (adverb) (35) .... *osoku*

lavatory .... *gofujō*

learn (22) .... *narau*

left (11) .... *hidari*

leg (18) .... *ashi*

leisurely .... *yukkuri*

lend (19) .... *kasu*

letter (16) .... *tegami*

lie (falsehood) .... *uso*

light, electric (8) .... *dentō*

light (in weight) (3) .... *karui*

lips (18) .... *kuchibiru*

little (small) (3) .... *chiisai*

lobster; shrimp .... *ebi*

long (3) .... *nagai*

long objects, word used in counting (23) .... *hon*

lower part (10) .... *shita*

lunch .... *hirugohan (hiruhan)*

M

magazine (6) .... *zasshi*

maid (9) .... *jochū*

make (22) .... *tsukuru*

make a mistake (17) .... *machigaeru*

male (4) .... *otoko*

man, a (4) .... *otoko*

many .... *takusan*

map .... *chizu*

March (26) .... *Sangatsu*

mat, reed (18) .... *tatami*

matted floor (18) ...... *tatami*

May (26) .... *Gogatsu*

meal (21) .... *gohan*

meaning .... *imi*

meat (32) .... *niku*

mend (34) .... *naosu*

middle .... *mannaka*

milk .... *gyūnyū*

minute (24) ....*fun*

Miss (4) .... *san*

mist .... *kiri*

Monday (25) .... *Getsuyōbi*

money (12) .... *okane*

moon (26) .... *tsuki*

more (26) .... *motto*

morning (8) .... *asa*

morning, this (6) .... *kesa*

most (26) .... *ichiban*

mother (12) .... *okāsan*

mother (the speaker's)
(19) .... *haha*

mountain .... *yama*

mouth (18) .... *kuchi*

move (31) .... *ugoku*

movie star (female) .... *jyoyū*

Mr. (4) .... *san*

Mrs. (4) .... *san*

much .... *takusan*

mushroom .... *kinoko*

music (22) .... *ongaku*

N

name (5) .... *namae*

narrow (3) .... *semai*

near (10) .... *soba*

near .... *chikai*

neck (18) .... *kubi*

need (17) .... *iru*

new (3) .... *atarashii*

newspaper (6) .... *shimbun*

next (25) .... *tsugi*

next day .... *yokujitsu*

night (8) .... *yoru*

nine (20; 23) ...... *kokonotsu; ku or kyū*

nine hundred (23) .... *kyūhyaku*

no (2) .... *iie*

No. 1 (26) .... *ichiban*

no good .... *dame*

noisy .... *yakamashii*

noon (8) .... *hiru*

no parking ..... *chūsha kinshi*

north (36) .... *kita*

nose (18) .... *hana*

no smoking .... *kin en*

notebook (1) .... *chōmen*

November (26) .... *Jūichigatsu*

now (8) .... *ima*

O

ocean .... *umi*

o'clock (24) .... *ji*

October (26) .... *Jūgatsu*

office (22) .... *jimusho*

officer .... *shōkō*

often .... *tabitabi*

old (of persons) ... *toshiyori no*

old (of things) (4) .... *furui*

older brother (32)ani; niisan

older sister (32) .... *ane; nēsan*

old man (35) .... *ojiisan*

on (10) .... *ni*

one (numeral)
(20; 23) .... *hitotsu; ichi*

one (pronoun) (35) .... *no*

one hundred (23) ...... *hyaku*

one person (23) .... *hitori*

one way .... *ippō kōtsū*

one week .... *isshūkon*

open (verb) (16) .... *akeru*

ornament (18) .... *okimono*

outside .... *soto*

overcoat .... *gaitō*

oyster .... *kaki*

P

package (12) .... *tsutsumi*

pagoda, five story
(9) .... *gojūnotō*

painful .... *itai*

painting (8) .... *e*

paper (1) .... *kami*

park .... *kōen*

peach (13) .... *momo*

peculiar .... *hen (na)*

pen, fountain (2) .... *mannenhitsu*

pencil (1) .... *empitsu*

people (4) .... *hitobito*

people, word used in counting more than two (23) .... *nin*

pepper .... *koshō*

person (4) .... *hito; kata*

peruse (14) .... *yomu*

photograph (12) ..... *shashin*

picture (painting; sketch) (8) .... *e*

place .... *tokoro*

place, that (11) .... *soko*

place, that (over there) (11) .... *asoko*

place, this (11) .... *koko*

place, what? (11) .... *doko*

plate; dish (13) .... *sara*

play (drama) .... *shibai*

pleasant .... *tanoshii*

please (34) .... *dōzo*

please give me (34) .... *kudasai*

P.M. .... *gogo*

pocket book (2) .... *saifu*

policeman (9) .... *junsa*

police station .... *keisatsusho*

poor .... *bimbō (na)*

postage stamp (12) .... *kitte*

postcard .... *hagaki*

picture postcard ...... *ehagaki*

post office .... *yūbinkyoku*

pot (cooking) (9) .... *kama*

precious .... *taisetsu (na)*

pretty (6) .... *kirei (na)*

price (33) .... *nedan*

probably (21) .... *tabun*

pupil (6) .... *seito*

purse (2) .... *saifu*

Q

quick (adv.) (29) ...... *hayaku*

R

radio (22) .... *rajio*

railroad station (6) .... *eki*

rain (noun) (33) .... *ame*

rain (verb) .... *ame ga furu*

razor .... *kamisori*

read (14) .... *yomu*

rear (10) .... *ushiro*

red (4) .... *akai*

rest (verb) (25) .... *yasumu*

restaurant (large Japanese) (11) .... *ryōriya*

rice (cooked) (21) ...... *gohan*

rice bowl (9) .... *chawan*

right (direction) (11) .... *migi*

right away (33) .... *sugu*

ring .... *yubiwa*

river .... *kawa*

road (4) .... *michi*

room (3) .... *heya*

rush (17) .... *isogu*

Russia (6) .... *Roshiya*

Russian (language) (6) .... *Roshiyago*

Russian (native) (6) .... *Roshiyajin*

S

sad .... *kanashii*

sailor (9) .... *suihei*

salt .... *shio*

same .... *onaji*

samisen (15) .... *shamisen*

sandals (15) .... *zōri*

satchel (1) .... *kaban*

Saturday (25) .... *Doyōbi*

school (11) .... *gakkō*

scroll, hanging (18) .... *kakemono*

sea .... *umi*

second (part of minute)
(24) .... byō

secret .... himitsu

see (16) .... miru

sell (19) .... uru

send (19) .... okuru

September (26) ...... Kugatsu

sergeant (30) .... gunsō

seven (20; 23) .... nanatsu;
shichi or nana

seven hundred
(23) .... nanahyaku

shelf (18) .... tana

ship (13) .... fune

shirt (13) .... shatsu

shoes (2) .... kutsu

shop (store) .... mise

shop curtain (15) .... noren

short (3) .... mijikai

show (drama) .... shibai

shrimp .... ebi

shrine (9) .... omiya

sickness .... byōki

side (11) .... yoko

side (26) .... hō

silk .... kinu

since (24) .... kara

six (20; 23) ...... muttsu; roku

six hundred (23) ... roppyaku

skillful (6) .... jōzu (na)

sky .... sora

sleep .... nemuru

sleepy .... nemui

slow .... osoi

slowly .... yukkuri

small (3) .... chiisai

small (in area) (3) ..... semai

snow (noun) (33) .... yuki

snow (verb) ...... yuki ga furu

so (15) .... sō

soap .... sekken

soldier (9) .... heitai

sometimes .... *tokidoki*

son .... *musuko*

soon, very .... *sugu*

soup .... *suimono*

south (36) .... *minami*

speak (14) .... *hanasu*

spectacles (2) .... *megane*

spoon (20) .... *saji*

spring (season) (8) ...... *haru*

spring, hot .... *onsen*

stamp, postage .... *kitte*

stand (table) (10) .... *dai*

star .... *hoshi*

stomach (18) .... *hara*

store .... *mise*

straight (11) .... *massugu*

strange .... *hen (na)*

strawberry .... *ichigo*

street (4) .... *michi*

streetcar (24) .... *densha*

strong (sturdy) (6) .... *jōbu (na)*

study .... *benkyō suru*

subway .... *chikatetsu*

sugar .... *satō*

summer (8) .... *natsu*

sun .... *taiyō*

Sunday .... *Nichiyōbi*

T

table (2) .... *tēburu*

table, for eating, low
(15) .... *ozen*

take (time or money) ..... *kakaru*

take (carry a thing) ... *motte iku*

take (a person or
animal) .... *tsurete iku*

take a walk (33) ..... *sampo suru*

talk (14) .... *hanasu*

tangerine .... *mikan*

tea (green) .... *ocha*

teach (19) .... *oshieru*

teacher (8) .... *sensei*

tea kettle (9) .... *dobin*	*this (adjective) (4)* .... *kono*
telephone (12) .... *denwa*	*this month* .... *kongetsu*
ten (20; 23) .... *tō; jū*	*this place* .... *koko*
than (26) .... *yori*	*thousand (23)* .... *sen*
that (pronoun) (2) .... *sore*	*three (20; 23)* ..... *mittsu; san*
that (adjective) (4) .... *sono*	*three hundred (23)* ... *sanbyaku*
that (over there) (pronoun) (2) .... *are*	*Thursday (25)* ...... *Mokuyōbi*
	ticket .... *kippu*
that (over there) (adj.) (4) .... *ano*	*time (free)* .... *hima*
that place (11) .... *soko*	*time (24)* .... *jikan*
that place (over there) (11) .... *asoko*	*time, for tbe first (15)* .... *hajimete*
theater .... *gekijō*	*tired* .... *tsukareta*
theater, movie .... *eigakan*	*to (10)* .... *ni*
then (22) .... *sorekara*	*to (19)* .... *e*
there (11) .... *soko*	*tobacco tray (18)* ... *tabako-bon*
thing (abstract) .... *koto*	*today (14)* .... *kyō*
thing (concrete) .... *mono*	*together (21)* .... *issho ni*
thirteen (23) .... *jūsan*	*tomorrow (14)* .... *ashita*
thirty (23) .... *sanjū*	*tonight (21)* .... *komban*
this (pronoun) (1) .... *kore*	*too (26)* .... *mo*

too much (33) .... *amari*

tooth (18) .... *ha*

top (10) .... *ue*

torii (9) .... *torii*

toward (19) .... *e*

town (6) .... *machi*

train, steam (6) .... *kisha*

travel (noun) (35) .... *ryokō*

traveling bag (1) .... *kaban*

tray, tobacco (18) ... *tabako-bon*

tree (6) .... *ki*

trousers (13) .... *zubon*

truth .... *hontō*

Tuesday (25) .... *Kayōbi*

turn (become) (30) ...... *naru*

twelve (23) .... *jūni*

twenty (23) .... *nijū*

twenty-one (23) ...... *nijū-ichi*

twenty-two (23) .... *nijū-ni*

two (20; 23) .... *futatsu; ni*

two hundred (23) .... *nihyaku*

two people (23) .... *futari*

U

umbrella (9) .... *kasa*

under construction .... *kōji chū*

understand (17) .... *wakaru*

undesirable .... *kirai (na)*

unhappy .... *kanashii*

unhealthy (6) .... *yowai*

unskillful .... *heta (na)*

until; up to (24) .... *made*

usually .... *taitei*

V

vase (high) (18) .... *kabin*

vegetables .... *yasai*

very (30) .... *taihen*

very soon .... *sugu*

village .... *mura*

W

walk (verb) (32) .... *aruku*

wall (8) .... *kabe*

wallet (2) .... *saifu*

want (17) .... *iru*

war .... *sensō*

warm (7) .... *atatakai*

was (15) .... *deshita*

wash (verb) (34) .... *arau*

watch (time piece) (13) ..... *tokei*

water (cold) .... *mizu*

water (hot) .... *oyu*

watermelon .... *suika*

weak (6) .... *yowai*

weather (33) .... *tenki*

Wednesday (25) .... *Suiyōbi*

were (15) .... *deshita*

west (36) .... *nishi*

what? (15) .... *nani (nan)*

what day of the week? (25) .... *naniyōbi*

what kind of? (3) .... *donna*

when? (15) .... *itsu*

whenever (33) .... *to*

where? (11) .... *doko*

which (of two) (26) ... *dochira*

which (of three or more) (26) .... *dore*

white (3) .... *shiroi*

who? (5) .... *dare; donata*

why? .... *dōshite*

wide (3) .... *hiroi*

wife (the speaker's) (19) .... *kanai*

wife (someone else's) ... *okusan*

wind .... *kaze*

window (8) .... *mado*

winter (8) .... *fuyu*

wise (6) .... *rikō (na)*

with (21) .... *to*

with (22) .... *de*

woman, a (4) .... *onna no hito*

wooden (6) .... *ki no*

wooden clogs (15) .... *geta*

word (16) .... *kotoba*

*word used in counting
flat objects (23)* .... *mai*

*word used in counting
long objects (23)* .... *hon*

*word used in counting more
than two persons (23)* ...... *nin*

work (verb) (22) ...... *hataraku*

work .... *shigoto*

worry .... *shimpai*

wrist (18) .... *tekubi*

write (14) .... *kaku*

Y

yellow (4) .... *kiiroi*

yes (3) .... *hai*

yesterday (15) .... *kinō*

you (4) .... *anata*

young .... *wakai*

younger brother (32) ...... *otōto*

younger sister (32) ..... *imōto*

JAPANESE-ENGLISH VOCABULARY

The numerals in parentheses indicate the lessons in which the words are introduced. Words not followed by numerals have been added to those appearing in the lessons.

A

ageru (19) .... *give (to someone except the speaker)*

ago (18) .... *chin*

aida (10) .... *between*

akai (4) .... *red*

akambō (4) .... *baby*

akeru (16) .... *open (verb)*

aki (8) .... *autumn*

amari (33) .... *too much*

ame .... *candy*

ame (33) .... *rain (noun)*

ame ga furu .... *rain (verb)*

Amerika (4) .... *America*

Amerikajin (6) ..... *American*

anata (4) .... *you*

ane (32) .... *older sister*

ani (32) .... *older brother*

ano (4) .... *that (over there)*

annai .... *guide*

aoi (4) .... *blue*

arau (34) .... *wash (verb)*

are (2) .... *that (over there)*

aruku (32) .... *walk (verb)*

asa (8) .... *morning*

asagohan (asahan) (24) .... *breakfast*

asatte (21) .... *day after tomorrow*

ashi (18) .... *foot; leg*

ashikubi (18) .... *ankle*

ashita (14) .... *tomorrow*

asoko (11) .... *that place (over there)*

atama (18) .... *head*

atarashii (3) .... *fresh; new*

atatakai (7) .... *warm*

atena ..... *address (on a letter)*

atsui (7) .... *hot*

B

baka .... *fool*

baketsu (15) .... *bucket*

ban (8) .... *evening*

bangohan (22) .... *dinner (evening meal)*

bata (13) .... *butter*

benkyō suru .... *study*

bimbō (na) .... *poor*

bōshi(1) .... *cap; hat*

budō .... *grapes*

byō (24) .... *second (part of minute)*

byōin .... *hospital*

byōki .... *sickness*

C

chawan (9) .... *rice bowl*

chichi (19) .... *father (the speaker's)*

chiisai (3) .... *little; small*

chikai .... *near*

chikatetsu .... *subway*

chizu .... *map*

chōchin (9) .... *Japanese paper lantern*

chōmen (1) .... *notebook*

Chūgokugo (6) .... *Chinese (language)*

Chūgokujin (6) .... *Chinese (native)*

Chūgoku (6) .... *China*

chūsha kinshi .... *no parking*

D

dai (10) .... *stand (table)*

daidokoro (20) .... *kitchen*

daigaku .... *college*

daijōbu .... *all right*

dame .... *no good*

dansu (35) .... *dance*

dare (donata) (5) .... *who?*

de .... *See "Notes" for Lesson 22*

deguchi .... *exit*

dekakeru (25) .... *go out*

densha (24) .... *electric train; streetcar*

dentō (8) .... *electric light*

denwa (12) .... *telephone*

deru (24) .... *come out; depart, go out*

deshita (15) .... *was; were*

desu (1) .... *am; are; is*

dewa arimasen (2) ... *am not; are not; is not*

dobin (9) .... *pot; tea kettle*

dochira (26) .. *which (of two)*

doko (11) .... *what place?; where?*

dōmo (35) .... *indeed*

donna (3) .... *what kind of?*

dore (26) ..... *which? (of three or more)*

Doyōbi (25) .... *Saturday*

dōzo (34) .... *please*

e (8) .... *drawing, painting; picture*

e (19) .... *to; toward*

ebi .... *lobster; shrimp*

ehagaki .... *post card (picture)*

eigakan .... *movie theater*

Eigo (6) .... *English (lang.)*

eki (6) .... *railroad station*

empitsu (1) .... *pencil*

fue (15) .... *flute*

Fujisan (9) .... *Mt. Fuji*

fun (24) .... *minute*

fune (13) .... *boat; ship*

furo .... *bath*

furu (33) .... *fall (rain or snow) (verb)*

furui (4) .... *old (of things)*

fusuma (18) .... *heavy paper door*

futari (23) .... *two people*

futatsu (20) .... *two*

fūtō (12) .... *envelope*

futon ... *bed (Japanese style)*

fuyu (8) .... *winter*

gohan (21) .... *cooked rice; meal*

gohyaku (23) ... *five hundred*

gofujō .... *lavatory*

gojūnotō (9) .... *five-story pagoda*

gozen (24) ..... *A.M.; forenoon*

gunsō (30) .... *sergeant*

guntai .... *armed forces*

gyūnyū .... *milk*

G

gaitō .... *overcoat*

gakkō (11) .... *school*

gekijō .... *theater*

genki (na) ...... *healthy; high-spirited*

geta (15) .... *wooden clogs*

Getsuyōbi (25) .... *Monday*

ginkō .... *bank (for money)*

go (23) .... *five*

Gogatsu (26) .... *May*

gogo (24) .... *afternoon; P.M.*

H

ha (18) .... *tooth*

hachi (23) .... *eight*

Hachigatsu (26) .... *August*

hagaki .... *postcard*

haha (19) .... *mother (the speaker's)*

hai (3) .... *yes*

haizara .... *ashtray*

hajimete (15) .... *for the first time*

hako (1) .... *box*

hambun .... *half*

han (24) .... *half past*

hana (3) .... *flower*

hana (18) .... *nose*

hanasu (14) .... *speak; talk*

happyaku (23) .... *eight hundred*

hara (18) .... *abdomen; stomach*

haru (8) ...... *spring (season)*

hashi .... *bridge*

hashi (9) .... *chopsticks*

hata (4) .... *flag*

hataraku (22) ... *work (verb)*

hayai .... *early; fast (adj.)*

hayaku (29) .... *early; fast; quickly (adverb)*

heisha .... *barracks*

heitai (9) .... *soldier*

hen (na) .... *peculiar*

heta (na) .... *clumsy; unskillful*

heya (3) .... *room*

hi (25) .... *day*

hibachi (15) .... *fire brazier*

hidari (11) .... *left*

higashi .... *east*

hikōki (13) .... *airplane*

hima .... *free time*

himitsu .... *secret*

hiroi (3) .... *broad; large in area; wide*

hiru (8) .... *daytime; noon*

hirugohan (hiruhan) ...*lunch*

hitai (18) ....*forehead*

hito (kata) (4) .... *person*

hitobito (4) .... *people*

hitori (23) .... *one person*

hitotsu (20) ... *one (numeral)*

hō (26) .... *direction; side*

hoho (18) .... *cheek*

hōki (9) .... *broom*

hombako .... *bookcase*

hon (1) .... *book*

hon (23) .... *word used in counting long objects*

hontō .... *truth*

honya (22) .... *bookstore*

hoshi .... *star*

hoshii (35) .... *desirous of having*

hyaku (23) .... *one hundred*

I

ichi (23) .... *one (numeral)*

ichiban (26) ...... *most; No. 1*

ichiban ii; ichiban yoi ... *best*

Ichigatsu (26) .... *January*

ichigo .... *strawberry*

Igirisu (6) .... *England*

Igirisujin (6) ..... *Englishman*

ie (3) .... *house*

ii (yoi) (4) .... *good*

iie (2) .... *no*

iku (yuku) (14) .... *go*

ikutsu (20) .... *how many?*

ima (8) .... *now*

imi .... *meaning*

imōto (32) ..... *younger sister*

inaka ... *country (rural area)*

inu (2) .... *dog*

ippō kōtsū .... *one way*

iriguchi .... *entrance*

iru (17) .... *need, want*

isha (9) .... *doctor*

isogashii .... *busy*

isogu (17) .... *hurry; rush (verb)*

issho ni (21) .... *together*

isshūkan .... *one week*

isu (1) .... *chair*

itai .... *painful*

itsu (15) .... *when?*

itsumo .... *always*

itsutsu (20) .... *five*

J

jama (na) .... *bothersome*

ji (24) .... *o'clock*

jibiki (29) .... *dictionary*

jidōsha (5) ... *automobile; car*

jikan (24) .... *hour; time*

jimusho (22) .... *office*

jishin .... *earthquake*

jitensha (5) .... *bicycle*

jōbu (na) (6) .... *healthy; strong*

jochū (9) .... *maid*

jōdan .... *joke*

jōzu (na) (6) ..... *good at; skillful*

jū (23) .... *ten*

Jūgatsu (26) .... *October*

jūichi (23) .... *eleven*

Juichigatsu (26).... *November*

jūni (23) .... *twelve*

Jūnigatsu (26) .... *December*

Junsa (9)............. *policeman*

jūsan (23)................. *thirteen*

jyoyū .... *actress*

K

kaban (1) .... *briefcase; satchel; traveling bag*

kabe (8) .... *wall*

kabin (18) .... *vase (high)*

kado .... *corner (outside)*

kagi (13) ....*key*

kakaru .... *take (time or money); cost*

kakemono (18)......... *hanging scroll*

kaki .... *oyster*

kaku (14) .... *draw; write*

kama (9) ... *boiler; kettle; pot*

kami (1) .... *paper*

kami (18) ... *hair (on the head)*

kamisori .... *razor*

kanai (19) .... *wife (the speaker's)*

kanari (30).................. *fairly*

kanashii .... *unhappy; sad*

kani .... *crab*

kao (18) .... *face*

kara (24) .... *from; since*

karanda (18) .... *body*

karui (3) ..... *light (in weight)*

kasa (9) .... *umbrella*

kashisotsu .... *enlisted man*

kasu (19) .... *lend*

kata .... *person*

kau (16) .... *buy*

kawa .... *river*

kawaii .... *cute*

Kayōbi (25) .... *Tuesday*

kaze .... *wind*

kaze .... *cold (in head)*

keisatsusho .... *police station*

kekkō .... *excellent; fine*

kentō .... *boxing*

kesa (6) .... *this morning*

ki (6) .... *tree*

kiiroi (4) .... *yellow*

kiku (22) .... *hear*

kin en .... *no smoking*

ki no (6) .... *wooden*

kinō (15) .... *yesterday*

kinoko .... *mushroom*

kinu .... *silk*

Kinyōbi (25) .... *Friday*

kippu .... *ticket*

kirai (na) .... *displeasing; undesirable*

kirei (na) (6) .... *clean; fine looking; pretty*

kiri ....*fog; mist*

kirométoru .... *kilometer*

kisha (6) .... *steam train*

kita .... *north*

kitte (12) .... *postage stamp*

kōba .... *factory*

kodomo (ko) (4) .... *child*

kōen .... *park*

kōfuku .... *happy*

kōji chū .... *under construction*

koko (11) ..... *here; this place*

kokonotsu (20) .... *nine*

komban (21) .... *tonight*

kongetsu .... *this month*

kono (4) .... *this*

koppu (13) .... *drinking glass*

kore (1) .... *this*

kōri .... *ice*

koshō .... *pepper*

koto .... *thing (abstract)*

kotoba (16) .... *word*

ku (23) .... *nine*

kubi (18) .... *neck*

kuchi (18) .... *mouth*

kuchibiru (18) .... *lips*

kudamono .... *fruit*

kudasai (34) ... *please give me*

Kugatsu (26) .... *September*

kuroi (3) .... *black*

kuru (14) .... *come*

kushi (9) .... *comb*

kusuriya .... *drugstore*

kutsu (2) .... *shoes*

kyō (14) .... *today*

kyōkai .... *church*

kyū (23) .... *nine*

kyūhyaku (23) .... *nine hundred*

kyūkō .... *express train*

M

machi (6) .... *town*

machigaeru (17) .... *make a mistake*

made (24) ..... *as far as; until; up to*

mado (8) .... *window*

mae (10; 24) .... *before; front*

mai (23) .... *word used in counting flat objects*

mai (25) .... *every (prefix)*

mainichi .... *every day*

manaita .... *cutting board*

mannaka .... *middle*

mannenhitsu (2) ..... *fountain pen*

massugu (11) .... *straight*

mata .... *again*

mawari michi .... *detour*

me (18) .... *eye*

megane (2) .... *spectacles*

michi (4) .... *road; street*

midori (4) .... *green*

migi (11) .... *right (direction)*

mijikai (3) .... *short*

mikan .... *tangerine*

mimi (18) .... *ear*

minami .... *south*

minna (23) ...... *all; everybody; everything*

miru (16) .... *see*

mise .... *shop; store*

mittsu (20) .... *three*

mizu .... *water (cold)*

mizuumi .... *lake*

mo (26) .... *also; too*

mō (30) .... *already*

mochiron .... *certainly*

Mokuyōbi (25) ...... *Thursday*

momo (13) .... *peach*

mon .... *gate*

mono .... *thing (concrete)*

moshi (33) .... *if*

motsu (32) .... *have; held*

motte iku .... *carry; take (carry a thing)*

motto (26) .... *more*

mune (78) .... *breast; chest*

mura .... *village*

musuko .... *son*

musume .... *daughter*

muttsu (20) .... *six*

muzukashii (7) .... *difficult*

N

nagai (3) .... long

nagagutsu (15) ... long boots

naka (10) .... inside

namae (5) .... name

nampun .... how many minutes?

nan (15) .... what?

nana (23) .... seven

nanatsu (20) .... seven

nanahyaku (23) .... seven hundred

nani (15) .... what?

naniyōbi (25) .... what day of the week?

naosu (34) .... fix; mend

nara (33) .... if

narau (22) .... learn

naru (30) ... become; get; turn

natsu (8) .... summer

nedan (33) .... price

neko (2) .... cat

nemui .... sleepy

nemuru .... sleep

nēsan (32) .... older sister

ni (10) .... at; in; on; to

ni (23) .... two

nichi (25) .... day (in compounds)

Nichiyōbi (25) .... Sunday

Nigatsu (26) .... February

Nihon; Nippon (6) .... Japan

Nihongo; Nippongo (6) ...... Japanese (language)

Nihonjin; Nipponjin (6) .... Japanese (native)

Nihyaku (23) ... two hundred

niisan (32) ..... older brother

nijū (23) .... twenty

nijū-ichi (23) ..... twenty-one

nijū-ni (23) .... twenty-two

niku (32) .... meat

nin (23) .... word used in counting more than two persons

nishi .... *west*

no (35) .... *one (pronoun)*

no (5) .... *of (particle)*

nomu (14) .... *drink*

no naka (26) .... *among*

noren (15) .... *shop curtain*

nurimono .... *lacquerware*

O

ocha .... *green tea*

odori .... *dance*

oishii .... *delicious*

ojiisan (35) .... *old man*

okane (12) .... *money*

okāsan (12) .... *mother*

okashi (19) .... *cake*

ōkii (3) .... *big; large*

okimono (18) .... *ornament*

okiru (25) .... *get up*

okuru (19) .... *send*

omiya (9) .... *shrine*

omoi (3) .... *heavy*

omoshiroi (6) ... *entertaining; interesting*

onaji .... *same*

ongaku .... *music*

onna (4) ... *female; a woman*

onsen .... *hot spring*

oshieru (19) .... *teach*

osoi .... *late; slow*

osoku (35) .... *late (adverb)*

otoko (4) .... *male; a man*

otōsan (12) .... *father*

otōto (32) ... *younger brother*

oyu .... *water (hot)*

ozen (15) .... *low table for eating*

P

pan (13) .... *bread*

R

rajio (22) .... *radio*

renga (29) .... *brick*

rikō (na) (6) .... *clever; intelligent; wise*

ringo (13) .... *apple*

roku (23) .... *six*

Rokugatsu (26) .... *June*

roppyaku (23) ... *six hundred*

Roshiya (6) .... *Russia*

Roshiyago (6) .... *Russian (language)*

Roshiyajin (6) .... *Russian (native)*

ryokan .... *hotel (Japanese style)*

ryokō (35) .... *travel (noun)*

ryōria (11) .... *restaurant (large Japanese)*

S

saifu (2) .... *pocketbook; purse; wallet*

saji (20) .... *spoon*

sakana (3) .... *fish*

sakuban (15) .... *last evening*

sakura (9) ... *cherry blossom*

sampo suru (33) ... *take a walk*

samui (7) ..... *cold (weather)*

san (4) .... *Mr.; Mrs.; Miss*

san (23) .... *three*

sanbyaku (23) .... *three hundred*

Sangatsu (26) .... *March*

sanjū (23) .... *thirty*

sara (13) .... *dish; plate*

satō .... *sugar*

seito (6) .... *pupil*

sekken .... *soap*

semai (3) .... *narrow; small in area*

sen (23) .... *thousand*

sensei (8) .... *teacher*

sensō .... *war*

sensu (15) .... *folding fan*

shamisen (15) .... *samisen*

shashin (12) ...... *photograph*

shashinki (4) .... *camera*

shatsu (13) .... *shirt*

shi .... city

shi (23) .... four

shibai .... drama (play)

shichi (23) .... seven

Shichigatsu (26) .... July

Shigatsu (26) .... April

shigoto .... job; work

shijū (23) .... forty

shima .... island

shimbun (6) .... newspaper

shimeru (16) ..... close (verb)

shimpai .... anxiety; worry

shindai (10) ..... bed (western style)

shinsetsu (na) .... kind

shio .... salt

shiroi (3) .... white

shita (10) .... bottom; lower part

shitamachi .... downtown

shōbōsho .... fire station

shōji (18) .... light paper door

shōkō .... officer

so (15) .... so

soba (10) .... near

soko (11) ... that place; there

sono (4) .... that (adjective)

sora .... sky

sore (2) .... that (pronoun)

sorekara (22) ..... afterwards; then

soto .... outside

sugi (24) .... after

sugu (33) .... at once; immediately; right away; very soon

suihei (9) .... sailor

suika .... watermelon

suimono .... soup

Suiyōbi (25) .... Wednesday

suki ....fond (of)

sukiyaki (35) .... Japanese meat & vegetable dish

sumi .... *corner (inside)*

suru (21) .... *do*

suzushii (7) .... *cool (weather)*

T

tabako-bon (18) .... *tobacco tray*

tabemono ....*food*

taberu (14) .... *eat*

tabitabi .... *often*

tabun (21) .... *probably*

tachi .... *plural suffix for persons*

takai (4) ...... *expensive; high*

take .... *bamboo*

taihen .... *very*

taii (30) .... *captain*

taisetsu (na) .... *important; precious*

taitei .... *usually*

taiyō .... *sun*

tamago .... *egg*

tana (18) .... *shelf*

tanoshii .... *enjoyable; pleasant*

tansu (11) .... *chest of drawers*

tatami (18) ...... *matted-floor; reed mat*

tatemono .... *building*

tateru (29) .... *build*

te (11) .... *hand*

tēburu (2) .... *table*

tegami (16) .... *letter*

tekubi (18) .... *wrist*

tempura (35) .... *Japanese meat or fish deep fry*

tenjō (8) .... *ceiling*

tenki (33) .... *weather*

to (8) .... *door*

to (13) .... *and*

to (21) .... *with*

to (33) .... *whenever*

tō (20) .... *ten*

todana (13) .... *closet*

tōi .... *distant; far*

tokei (13) .... *watch; clock*

tokidoki .... *sometimes*

tokonoma (18) .... *alcove*

tokoro .... *place*

tokoya .... *barber*

tomodachi (14) .... *friend*

tori (11) .... *bird*

torii (9) .... *torii*

tōrō (9) .... *stone or metal lantern*

toshiyori no .... *old (of persons)*

tōtō (30) ....*finally*

tsugi (25) .... *next*

tsukareta .... *tired*

tsuki .... *moon*

tsuku (15) .... *arrive*

tsukue (1) ....*desk*

tsukuru (22) .... *make*

tsurete iku ...... *take (a person or animal)*

tsutsumi (12) .... *bundle; package*

tsuzumi (15) ...... *drum, hand*

U

uchi (12) .... *home*

uchiwa (15) .... *non-folding fan*

ude (18) .... *arm*

ue (10) .... *above; on; top*

ugoku (31) .... *move*

uma (12) .... *horse*

umi .... *ocean; sea*

uru (19) .... *sell*

ushiro (10) .... *rear*

uso ....*falsehood; lie*

utsukushii (3) .... *beautiful*

W

wakai .... *young*

wakaru (17) .... *understand*

warui (4) .... *bad*

wasureru (16) .... *forget*

watakushi; wata'shi (4) ...... *I*

Y

yakamashii .... *noisy*

yama .... *mountain*

yasai .... *vegetables*

yasashii (7) .... *easy*

yasui (4) .... *cheap;
inexpensive*

yasumu (25) .... *go to bed; rest*

yattsu (20) .... *eight*

yoii (ii) (4) .... *good*

yoko (11) .... *side*

yokujitsu .... *next day*

yomu (14) .... *peruse; read*

yon (23) .... *four*

yonhyaku (23) .... *four hundred*

yonjū (23) .... *forty*

yori (26) .... *than*

yoru (8) .... *night*

yottsu (20) .... *four*

yowai (6) ... *unhealthy; weak*

yūgata (8) ... *toward evening*

yūbinkyoku .... *post office*

yubiwa .... *ring*

yuka (8) .... *floor*

yuki (33) .... *snow (noun)*

yuki ga furu ...... *snow (verb)*

yukkuri ...... *slowly, leisurely*

yuku .... *go*

Z

zabuton (18) .... *cushion*

zasshi (6) .... *magazine*

zōri (15) .... *sandals*

zubon (13) .... *trousers*

How to use this CD-ROM for Japanese

This CD-ROM includes games, tutors, and utilities that will enrich the experience of learning about Japanese language and culture. Most of the applications included on the CD-ROM focus on learning the Japanese writing systems, kanji, katakana, and hiragana. As you begin your study of the Japanese language, these applications will help you deepen your understanding of written and spoken Japanese, as well as assist you in tracking your progress. As your fluidity with the language increases, you will find new challenges in the software, complementing your study of the text.

To begin, open the file entitled OPENME.HTML in your favorite Web browser, such as Microsoft Internet Explorer or Netscape Navigator. This file will provide an overview of the applications included on the CD-ROM.

Microsoft Internet Explorer users may install the applications by simply clicking on their icons. This will initiate the installation process. When prompted, choose to open the file from its current location.

Netscape Navigator users may view the HTML file to get more information about each application. When you have chosen the applications you would like to install, follow the steps below:

1. Double-click on the My Computer icon on your desktop.

2. Right-click on the CD-ROM icon in the My Computer window, and choose "Explore."

3. Double-click on the shortcut that corresponds to the program you would like to install.

For more information about the developers of each application, view the "Links" page in your favorite Web browser. Please note that a browser is not required to install the applications on the CD-ROM. If you prefer not to use a Web browser, you can install any or all of the applications included by following the steps above.